Policy and Practice

The Experience
of Government

ROYAL INSTITUTE OF PUBLIC ADMINISTRATION

First published in 1980

This book is copyright under the Berne Convention. All rights are reserved. Apart from any fair dealing for the purpose of private study, research, criticism or review, as permitted under the Copyright Act 1956, no part of this publication may be reproduced, stored in a retrieval system, or transmitted, in any form or by any means, electronic, electrical, chemical, mechanical, optical, photocopying, recording or otherwise, without the prior permission of the copyright owner. Inquiries should be addressed to the publishers.

© Royal Institute of Public Administration, 1980.

'Manifestos and Mandarins' © Tony Benn.

Cover photographs of Shirley Williams, Tony Benn, William Rodgers, and Merlyn Rees by permission of *The Guardian*; Edmund Dell courtesy of Keystone Press Agency, Ltd.

Cartoons on page 76 and 85
by permission of
Les Gibbard, *The Guardian*.

Published by the Royal Institute of Public Administration,
3 Birdcage Walk, London SW1H 9JJ.
Printed in England by Victoria House Printing Co.,
25 Cowcross Street, London EC1

ISBN 0 900628 21 9

Contents

Introduction

A major problem faced by students of British central government is that so much of the information about what goes on inside Whitehall is unreliable, incomplete, based entirely on outside information, out-of-date, or some combination of these. Serving Ministers and civil servants do not normally talk in public about the nature of their jobs. Retired civil servants rarely write their memoirs; when former Ministers write theirs, they tend to concentrate more on politics than on administration. The latter tends to be treated mainly in terms of the relatively glamorous end-products of the process, such as the great parliamentary occasion, the opening of the millionth house or the climax of an international negotiation. Exceptionally, Richard Crossman was concerned to set down his view of what it was "really like" in Whitehall, but by the accident of fate he was no longer available to discuss his account when it was published.

The Royal Institute of Public Administration, which has a long and successful tradition of sponsoring public lectures, therefore took the chance offered by the defeat in May 1979 of the incumbent Labour Government to invite six senior members of that Government to talk to RIPA audiences about their own experiences in office, while these were still fresh in their minds. (One of the speakers, Mr. Edmund Dell, had in fact resigned from the Cabinet and from Parliament some months before the election.)

The lectures were delivered between November 1979 and March 1980, early on weekday evenings in the large lecture hall at the Royal Institute of International Affairs in St. James's Square, London. Each attracted a large and clearly interested audience, consisting of RIPA members and a few invited guests. There was no shortage of questions for the speakers after each talk (which came mainly, but by no means exclusively, from civil servants). Both the content of the lectures and the interest they aroused showed clearly that the RIPA had been right in supposing that former Ministers would have something important to say about the business of government. The RIPA is grateful to the speakers for agreeing in this way to increase the sum of public knowledge and understanding of how Whitehall does, or should, work, and for allowing their talks now to be published for the benefit of a wider audience.

William Plowden

Westminster and Whitehall: Adapting to Change

WILLIAM RODGERS

Some years ago, I suggested to the head of an Oxford college that there might be merit in a weekend seminar bringing together Ministers, ex-Ministers and civil servants of differing levels of experience, to discuss the problems of government. I believe that he consulted a senior politician who was then a visiting fellow of the college before turning the idea down.

Fashions change and I greatly welcome the thought behind this series of lectures, although about my own role I have felt growing doubt. In retrospect, it would have been far wiser to concern myself with a limited field in which my experience would have been in some way special and, as a result, more interesting. I am only too aware that I shall be covering familiar ground and contributing to a debate that will continue as long as we have our present form of government. In practice, I shall not be discussing in detail or in depth changes accomplished or required in Westminster amongst parliamentarians, or in Whitehall amongst civil servants. I shall be mainly considering what I suppose should be called the "interface" between Ministers and civil servants, particularly what is often called "the mandarin class".

This relationship is without obvious parallels elsewhere. Members of Parliament become Ministers often without any experience of administration, least of all in running a large organization. Except in wartime, civil servants very rarely become Ministers themselves. Yet it is rare, except in the intimacy of a Private Office, for discussion to take place about how Ministers and civil servants can best work together. It is taken for granted that they are obliged to do so and should get on with it.

The great fascination of the Crossman diaries is that they take the lid off this relationship in the context of events as they are supposed to have happened. The drawback, of course, is that one man's experience is then regarded as typical, while every Minister is different — and Dick Crossman was more different than most.

I remember writing to him when he was Minister of Housing and I was a Parliamentary Under-Secretary in DEA. I was dealing with regional policy under George Brown and it seemed natural for me to write direct to Dick Crossman because I had known him personally for many years. When no reply came, I asked my Private Secretary to telephone the Minister's Private Office to discover what had happened. He was then told that Mr. Crossman would be replying to Mr. Brown because Cabinet Ministers could only correspond with colleagues of the same rank.

When I later taxed Dick Crossman with this story, he protested that his Private Secretary had told him that he wasn't allowed to write to a junior Minister. There are those who would say that this reveals the rigid sense of hierarchy that characterizes the civil service. But others might say that it reveals a Minister over-ready on this occasion to take "no" for an answer.

I mention this because it shows how the perspective — perhaps the character — of the individual Minister affects his judgment of the civil service with which he comes into contact.

I should therefore say now that I look back on almost all my eleven years of government as happy ones. During this time, I came to respect the great majority of the civil servants with whom I had to deal and to regard some with real affection. With few exceptions, they were able, hard-working and loyal. My frustrations and disappointments stemmed far more from the inevitable conflicts of politics and politicians.

But I fully recognize that my good fortune may have resulted from my having the style and temperament that civil servants tend to find least unacceptable in a Minister — and "getting on with civil servants" may arouse suspicions as a ministerial qualification. I make this as an entirely genuine point. There may be a need to redress the balance of what I have to say.

The question "How can Whitehall best serve Westminster?" is not new. Almost forty years ago, G.D.H. Cole, soon to become Chichele Professor of Social and Political Theory at Oxford, addressed the Fabian Society on "Reform in the Civil Service" — in a lecture still worth reading. Not long after, from a very different political point of view, L.S. Amery committed himself on the need for change in his "Thoughts on the Constitution". But it is in the last decade or so that there has been the flood. There have been Fulton, reports from the Expenditure Committee of the House of Commons, an endless debate arising from changes in the structure of government, the memoirs of a Prime Minister and the diaries of a Cabinet Minister — and much gossip dressed up as history (on the assumption that if you get in first, you create the legend). Within Whitehall itself, there has been a continuing flow of paper reviewing the training and recruitment of civil servants. No doubt CSD is, at this very moment, preparing a fresh announcement. What is there new to be said that will escape being dismissed as trivial and superficial because it is said in less than a hundred thousand words?

But if what I say reveals prejudices and views thought incompletely through, that fact itself may have some relevance. It is often the perception of the truth, not the truth itself, that matters.

First, may I make one comment about changes in the relationship of Ministers to one another? I cannot, of course, judge the behaviour of Ministers in the present Administration, but over my years in government (1964-1979) — with a gap in the middle — there was a significant growth of informality between Ministers and much less emphasis on status. This had its consequences for the relationship of Ministers to Parliament.

As a newcomer at a junior level in 1964, I found the hierarchy distasteful. In a significant sense, all Members of Parliament are equal, each having stood for election and reached the House of Commons on merit. But in government, it turned out to be different. There were top-dogs and dogs-bodies, the insiders and those who fetched and carried.

The fact is that a junior Minister is a political eunuch. He has lost the power to speak out boldly and to influence events, to be creative in the broad political arena.

It is to the Prime Minister that political power accumulates in office, quite out of proportion to the share enjoyed by the Leader when in Opposition. In this particular respect, the position today is as it was fifteen years ago when I found it a surprise and very frustrating. But in terms of identifiable roles and defined responsibilities and acceptance of them by the House of Commons, there has been a change.

A quarter of a century ago, Herbert Morrison set out what he called a "charter" for Parliamentary Secretaries and described the problems he had experienced — with his officials — in seeking to give them clear, delegated responsibilities. He also commented on the relatively new institution of the Minister of State, the role appropriate to him. I am sure that some Parliamentary Secretaries still have little work of their own and that some Permanent Secretaries prefer it that way (and would prefer fewer junior Ministers). But this is very much less the case than fifteen years ago and, as a result, the conduct of government — with its heavier burdens — is better than it would otherwise be.

As for the House of Commons, I confess that I was sceptical whether it would come to accept anyone less than the head of the department for an authentic view on great issues. But Ministers of State and most Parliamentary Secretaries are now given specific responsibilities, of which all MPs are informed, and even titles, by which they are known to the public. We have had a Minister for the Disabled, who was a Parliamentary Secretary; we have a Minister for Sport, who *is* a Parliamentary Secretary. We have, or have had, Ministers of State for Planning and Local Government, Housing and

Construction, Companies, Aviation and Shipping, Consumer Affairs. It is accepted that they should make Statements in the House and answer Private Notice Questions. The policy which they defend is seen as *their* policy or the policy of the Cabinet, not mainly the policy of the Secretary of State in whose department they serve.

I welcome this change. Although Mrs. Thatcher's Cabinet is larger than, say, Mr. Attlee's, there are fewer separate departments in Whitehall. In these circumstances, it is right that opportunities should exist for Ministers to carry real responsibility within a department and in the House of Commons long before becoming a department head.

But there is another change I would not welcome at all. Rather over ten years ago, the conglomerate or jumbo department became all the rage. This was at a time when most people seemed to believe that bigness was best and that government should model itself on the great industrial corporations. The motive was described as "efficiency" and the mood persisted into the first half of the 1970s. A team of knowledgeable tycoons roamed Whitehall and advised on how the failure of politicians and civil servants could be redeemed by the mysteries of modern management.

I am sure that there were useful by-products. Whitehall is dangerously inbred. Civil servants should be more exposed to — and more often drawn from — other walks of life. There are certainly some lessons to be learnt from the business world. But I sensed at the time that there was too great a readiness to draw parallels between a large manufacturing or retail business run by a chairman or chief executive and answerable to an annual meeting of shareholders (in a London hotel and lasting half-an-hour) and a government department whose Minister must answer daily to the House of Commons. The motives, objectives and responsibilities were very different.

I hope that we are not in for another comparable period of half-baked change in the name of efficiency. I said earlier that Ministers often achieved high office without any experience of administration. It is right that they should do so. Ministers are appointed mainly because of their understanding of Parliament and their representative role in their party. As we all know, few Ministers brought in directly from outside because of their assumed business acument have proven a success.

In my view, it would be a serious mistake if in some way Ministers were given new and extensive responsibilities for the day-to-day management of their departments, including the scale and efficiency of their executive operations. I do not believe that their talents and training suit them for this task or that they could accommodate the extra burden. It would certainly be quite indefensible if any such change took Ministers away from the House of Commons. Many of them spend too little time there already.

May I make clear that I do not rule out some new form of external efficiency audit, perhaps related mainly to manpower. In this respect, there is an interesting suggestion — or at least the embryo of one — in the recent report of the Spierenburg review body to the European Commission. There may be a case for slimming down Whitehall and advice on this — dare I say, from another quango? — could make sense. My objection is to treating Ministers as if they are — or should be — businessmen and the parliamentary process like a huge manufacturing or marketing operation. What is good for the supermarket is not necessarily good for Westminster and Whitehall.

Let me turn next to the question of civil service loyalty to Ministers, an old issue but one which persists, together with its variant that civil servants seek to thwart their Ministers from time to time.

Now there was an occasion very early in my ministerial career when, as a junior Minister, I found that a decision I had made was not being carried out by officials. When I asked why, the Assistant Secretary concerned said that she had not been sure whether my mind was made up or that the Secretary of State would endorse my view. I was angry, but, in retrospect, I do not think that her conduct was that unreasonable, given my newness to office and the personalities involved.

Nevertheless — and this is an important point — I believe that the civil service has very particular obligations towards Ministers new to a department, both in supporting them and ensuring that their wishes are carried out. There are many pitfalls to a stranger in the early stages of his ministerial career.

Another experience may illustrate this. As some of you will recall, the Department of Economic Affairs was a curious body with very limited executive responsibilities. It was, in a sense, the personal office of the First Secretary of State, George Brown — I refer to its earlier days. As a result, we muscled in on everyone's business. There was to be a debate on Northern Ireland and the First Secretary insisted that, in view of DEA's responsibilities for regional policy, I should wind it up. This was a disaster. Home Office officials were hostile because we were poaching on their ground. My own officials were not happy at offending another department, less than eager about extra work and understandably ill-informed about wider aspects of the Northern Ireland problem. As the victim, I felt badly let down.

I thus learnt the lesson that the loyalty of officials does not normally extend to a Minister in another department. And I have been very wary of dual departmental responsibility for parliamentary business ever since.

There is another, more obvious, area in which a Minister should be wary and where civil service mechanisms may not always prove an adequate corrective. I refer to the equivalent of "going native" for an expatriate serving in a foreign post. In my experience, there are occasions when an official gets too close to the interest group — or lobby — with which he deals and becomes instinctively resistant to ministerial proposals hostile to it. It is important that personnel policies should recognize this and strike the right balance, granted the advantages of some continuity in a post.

But there are a number of other ways in which the idea of "disloyalty" is unfairly invoked against the civil service. These are times when Ministers themselves must be capable of adjusting to and taking account of what seem to me to be the inevitable consequences of a career civil service.

In the first place, as civil servants have minds of their own — and are expected to have rather good ones — it would be quite unnatural for them to accept the view of a Minister without judging the merits of the issue themselves. In any case, this is precisely what they are meant to do in giving advice. Frequently, the line between one decision and another is fine and the balance of argument narrow. Agreement is relatively painless. But occasionally a Minister may take a view contrary to strong official advice on a major matter of policy where much is at stake. In this case, a Minister must credit and understand the strength of his officials' views and not resent an attempt to reopen the matter.

Secondly — although this begs some questions — it is inevitable with a career civil service, well established rules and a substantial element of continuity, that officials should occasionally look elsewhere — especially to the Treasury or Number 10 — for allies on a matter of importance. It may be to protect the Minister himself from the Prime Minister's wrath or to avoid a confrontation in committee. It may also be a rearguard action of a less defensible kind. But an experienced Minister should be aware that a "Whitehall mafia" — Hugh Gaitskell called it "the underground civil service" — is bound to exist and to use his wits accordingly.

The third possible infraction of loyalty is of a more serious kind. Put briefly, there is a temptation to discourage any action that may pre-empt the future when a new Administration is in prospect or create an irreversible situation in a controversial area. There are clear conventions in the period between a dissolution and the election of a new Parliament, although some tension between the Minister and his senior officials may be difficult to avoid. But there are other occasions when the active and instinctive loyalty of officials may be qualified either by a delicate parliamentary situation or a serious national crisis.

I have no solution to this except to say that a Minister must rise above his sense of frustration; try to understand the human factor; grit his teeth and press ahead if he believes he is right. I certainly cannot see how any change in structure or organization could improve matters. It is time to take the strain. I know that some senior civil servants become seriously concerned about accusations of disloyalty to Ministers. But I am doubtful whether criticism on this score is more commonplace today than, say, twenty-five years ago. Members of any outgoing administration, having lost an election, are certain to look for scapegoats: Ministers in a new administration are bound to be wary of those who advised their predecessors. It is certainly not the extent of criticism but its infrequency that usually strikes the observer from abroad.

I cannot accept the argument that, in some way, the civil service should redress the balance with a Minister who is inadequate to his task, as has lately been suggested, even to the extent of becoming the custodian of the manifesto on which he has fought an election.

Nor do I believe that a determined Minister will fail to get his way — provided that he is supported by his colleagues and, in the last analysis, by the Prime Minister. He should be capable of resisting the man-management of his Permanent Secretary, however skilful. He should have a clear view on how papers should be prepared and which of them he personally intends to study. He should become familiar with the committee system and how it can serve or frustrate him. Above all, he should be wary of being deodorized into a Whitehall figure-head without the distinctive taste and flavour of the experienced politicians. These obligations lie with him and no one else. He should not blame the civil service when he falls short.

I am referring here essentially to an established Secretary of State. I have previously mentioned the particular responsibility of the civil service towards a new Minister who does not yet know the ropes. I will just add that the complaints that junior Ministers have about officials should sometimes be directed to their own senior ministerial colleagues who do not always give them support.

One final thought on the question of loyalty. I would be surprised if there are no new Ministers at present around Whitehall without some sense of frustration after six months in office. I would expect a good deal of grumbling about the difficulties of moving as far and as fast as their election manifesto promised. But political parties in opposition do not spend a great deal of time on detailed and careful policy making or necessarily address themselves to the real problems that confront a party in power. Politicians should not blame officials if there are more obstacles to the course they wish to pursue than were dreamt of in the Carlton Club or Smith Square.

But politicians do have the right to complain if officials are remote from the Palace of Westminster and have too little knowledge of what lies behind the electoral system. Let me comment on the attitude of the civil service to Parliament.

It is a commonplace that a Minister must struggle to escape from his department — except after 6 o'clock at night — for other than departmental duties. It is a seductive restraint upon him because he enjoys being a Minister and different from over five hundred other Members of Parliament. Question Time or a major debate in the House is another matter and a Minister's success is much enjoyed by those who witness it (although the Treasury and the Foreign Office are usually more concerned that the record is straight than that the Minister survives).

But I am not sure that the civil service as a whole, and some younger civil servants in particular, fully appreciate that a Minister's first duty is to Parliament. And that Parliament is and should be, in the fullest sense, sovereign.

I remember speaking to a course — near Regents Park, some ten years ago — of young men and women who had lately joined the civil service. I had never met such arrogance. They were about to run the country and Parliament was an irrelevance.

I do not draw rigid conclusions from that. Many of us are arrogant at 22 or 23. A number of those whom I knew at that age who joined the civil service certainly tended towards pomposity if not priggishness! But I would like to find a means by which every administrative trainee in the civil service — or at least every high flyer — spent six months of his or her early career in and about the House of Commons, not only in the Chamber but in the corridors, lobbies and bars. It might, incidentally, improve the drafting of answers to PQs and letters to Members, on neither of which the civil service shines. As for the most senior civil servants, there may be a lesson for them, too.

In and out of government, I have been a strong supporter of the extension of the select committee principle. This has been a minority view amongst those who have held senior ministerial office. In the Labour Party, the old conventional Right and the old conventional Left unite in believing that select committees are perfidy. But I was, for three years, the chairman of a sub-committee of the Expenditure Committee. And as a Minister, I have appeared on the other side of the table on Treasury, Defence and Transport business.

Of course, the civil service is unlikely to welcome select committees and exposure to them — although officials, when they are open and know their stuff, do much better than they expect. But they should begin to regard them as important as Question Time and recognize in their hearts that they can contribute to the better government of Britain.

A Permanent Secretary once said to me, "I am worried I am now obliged to put an Assistant Secretary full-time on Expenditure Committee business." His was, I recall, the largest department in Whitehall at that time. One Assistant Secretary was one in 150. I felt obliged to suggest that his priorities might be wrong.

I believe that over the years the new system of departmental select committees will have a significant effect on the relationship between Westminster and Whitehall. They are certainly more likely to lead to more open government than any other current set of proposals. They provide Members of Parliament who are anxious to move in that direction with real opportunity. They should be taken very seriously. What about the relationship of civil servants to the political process itself? This is a delicate question. But all civil servants ought to know how the process works, at grassroots. What does the Member of Parliament do in his constituency? What is his relationship to his local party and to industry and commerce and to the trade unions?

I said that the first duty of a Minister was to Parliament. But before that in time, there is the party nomination and the votes of thousands of electors.

How many civil servants have attended the monthly meeting of the general management committee of a constituency Labour Party or the equivalent body in a local Conservative or Liberal Association? How many have been to an MP's surgery or joined an MP as he goes round a housing estate? For the most part, civil servants are remarkably sheltered from the political lives of Ministers. They miss an important dimension of the world of which they are part.

There is an easy remedy. Why not second civil servants at the appropriate time and level to MPs as Personal Assistants for, say, a period of six months? Not all MPs might welcome this, but I would be surprised if it were difficult to find, say, fifty back-benchers who would provide for short secondments. Young civil servants would get to know their way about Westminster. They would also do research and, most important, visit an MP's constituency. They would continue to be paid as civil servants. This is a better course than formal attachments to the staff of the House of Commons, although there may be scope for that, too.

Incidentally, the Annual Report of the Civil Service Commission for 1978 gives a list of 629 people who were invited to assist the Commission during the year by serving on selection boards or as examiners. There are professors, admirals, diplomats, bishops, even a journalist or two and someone described as "Mrs. M. Whitehouse". But there is not one Member of Parliament.

At this point, I would like to mention a related matter of current controversy. The Prime Minister has ordered an inquiry into quangos and Ministers are falling over each other in the rush to win credit by getting rid of them first. I do not wish to enter into this controversy in any significant way except to say that in my experience quangos do not proliferate in order to provide jobs for the boys. For the most part, there is too little talent available for unglamorous roles on the edge of government; and expert advice on specialized matters is usually worth having.

Perhaps I can establish my credentials here by saying that as Secretary of State I successfully resisted the proposal for a National Transport Council because I could not see how it would contribute to the solution of practical problems. The issues were too wide and too general to justify an advisory body, inevitably drawn mainly from both sides of the industry.

However, my anxiety lies in a different quarter. The fashionable era of the conglomerate department was also the era of hiving off — I do not mean industrial hiving-off from nationalized industries, which is a new and different matter. I played some part in this myself when, at the Board of Trade, we considered the organization of civil aviation in the aftermath of the Edwards Report. At that time, I was a hiver-offer, but I am far from sure now that I was right.

Do the Manpower Services Commission and ACAS function better outside a government department than within? Is the Health and Safety Executive more sensitive to public concern and faster to move in an emergency than when its functions were distributed round Whitehall? In hiving off, have we avoided altogether the duplication of personnel in residual departments? I am sure that the interest groups that largely seem to run these organizations would fight to safeguard their role. But when the CBI and the TUC are in alliance, my alarm bells begin to ring. In matters of public policy, responsibility to Ministers who are themselves responsible to Parliament has everything to recommend it. This is an area where I would like to turn back the clock at least a little. And any further proposals for hiving off will need the closest scrutiny.

I have mentioned the Manpower Services Commission and ACAS. For many years the old Ministry of Labour was a repository of much knowledge and wisdom about industrial relations. Officials actually knew the home telephone numbers of senior trade unionists and could even be seen having a drink with them round the corner from here in a pub near St. James's Square. In any industrial dispute, a sponsoring department would turn to the Ministry for advice and virtually bow out of subsequent developments. Perhaps conciliation too often meant splitting the difference and the style of the Ministry was unsuited to the harsher world of constant government involvement in incomes policy. Be that as it may, I believe that the public interest has suffered through the decline and dismemberment of the Ministry of Labour. It has not found a convincing new role nor have other departments that once relied upon it acquired their own industrial relations expertise.

This is a serious shortcoming in Whitehall and ought to be remedied if the Manpower Services Commission and ACAS are indeed gone for good. Every Minister in charge of a department should have a senior industrial relations adviser at his elbow. I do not necessarily say that he should be an outsider especially recruited to the service or available on temporary secondment. But he should be obliged to immerse himself in the subject thoroughly and be on familiar and friendly terms with senior people on both sides of industry.

I would also like to see a change in another area of specialist advise to Ministers: Information Officers. I have never understood why, at the most senior level, they are drawn from a separate class and not from the Administrative Division as a whole. Their role has become increasingly important, not only as advisers to Ministers, but in making policy comprehensible and effective amongst the public at large. Ministers have been served by some outstanding Information Officers. My personal experience has been a happy one and Number 10 has been amongst those generally served with skill and distinction. But I doubt whether the average quality satisfies most Ministers.

The Foreign Office approach is very different and I do not know why it cannot be followed elsewhere. The Head of Information, or his equivalent, is a high flyer in mid-career and he fills the position for two or three years. He may become the Secretary of State's Principal Private Secretary and he is certainly on his way to an important ambassadorial post. He holds regular press conferences and is generally held in high esteem by the knowledgeable journalists with whom he deals.

At a lower level, certain specialist skills may be required in a large information department. And I would not wish to impede in any way the progress of those who rise on merit through such a department to the top. In this case, however, the man or woman concerned should be capable of moving out of Information to another job elsewhere. I know that this happens very occasionally today. My case is for complete interchangeability, in effect, for one category or class at the top level.

There is a third area of advice to Ministers where I ask primarily for acceptance and consolidation. I refer to the role of Special Advisers. Almost forty years have passed since Hugh Dalton, newly appointed as Minister of Economic Warfare, invited the young Hugh Gaitskell, temporary civil servant and Labour candidate, to become what he called his *Chef de Cabinet*. The appointment was not popular with the Director-General of the Ministry. Later, when Dalton became President of the Board of Trade and Gaitskell went with him, there was another suspicious Permanent Secretary to be overcome. In the 1970s, the story has been repeated and I regret that many senior officials have been slow to accept this aspect of change. They see the Special Adviser as the cuckoo in the Whitehall nest.

I understand the hesitation. I was myself doubtful about the role of the Special Adviser until I was confronted with the task of running a

19

department. I then changed my mind and benefited very greatly from the help I received from the Special Adviser I chose. I should add that in this case, whatever initial reservations he may have had, my own Permanent Secretary showed the greatest kindness and helpfulness towards my Special Adviser. I am not aware that any serious problems arose concerning his role and status.

It may be said that the success of a Special Adviser depends upon the abilities and personality of the individual concerned and whether his relationship with the Minister damages or undermines the Minister's own relationship with his Private Office and Permanent Secretary. So be it: I accept that. I accept also that there should be some limit on the number of Special Advisers brought in by the Minister, although I am inclined to a larger team — perhaps 3 or 4 — than is currently assumed. But I believe that, in turn, others should accept — in the spirit as well as in the letter — that the Special Adviser, for those Ministers who want one, is a permanent and desirable feature of Whitehall.

In passing, can I pay tribute to that curious institution, unknown in other walks of life and without exact parallel in other forms of government, the Private Office? My first experience of a senior Minister's Private Office was perhaps unusual, in the sense that the Department of Economic Affairs under George Brown was unusual. But I learnt then of the extraordinary combination of skills that a good Private Secretary must possess, of which hard work, immense patience and infinite resilience are only the most obvious. I do not think that the role of the Private Secretary has been adequately described and assessed in any study of how government works. Here is yet another subject for a Ph.D. But one further thought. In the years ahead, every Private Secretary or, as a minimum, the Principal Private Secretary to a Head of Department, should have a competence in a Community language other than his own. The great majority of Private Secretaries have the ability to learn a language, often building very quickly on a residual knowledge. In due course, they would carry this ability into the highest ranks of the civil service where an older generation is, for the most part, remarkably lacking in languages. To be fair, I should add that an older generation of politicians is in much the same boat!

I want to turn finally and briefly to two related matters discussed by the Fulton Committee which remain central questions of concern. On this occasion, I can do little more than express my view without much elaboration. I have in mind the issues of movement into and out of the civil service and the controversy about generalists and specialists.

My own evidence to Fulton was not distinguished. As I recall, most of it was concerned with making the case against anyone being retained in the then Administrative Class who had not been promoted above Principal by the age of 40.

This was a rather blinkered view that I have since revised. But the idea of movement into and out of the service at every age and level has strong attractions. The vast majority of high flyers may join in their twenties, clear in their minds and dedicated to their chosen careers. But there should be no subsequent barrier to anyone who, on merit, deserves to be recruited. It follows that the civil service should be free to shed those who do not make the grade and might be much happier and more successful as the result of a mid-career change.

Some may join the civil service late with a view to remaining until their retirement. But why should it not be possible to join for two years or for five, to leave the service and return some years later, perhaps again on a temporary basis? I do not want to draw loose comparisons with experience in the United States because theirs is a different system of government. And I do not dismiss the possibility of a penalty, perhaps in the direction of some loss of integrity in the service. But the senior civil service needs some freshening and livening up. Civil servants spend too much time working with people whose career experience is largely identical.

This brings me to the question of specialization. Here I am old-fashioned and a heretic in the face of the conventional wisdom. I know that Fulton did not say that a third class degree in economics or in engineering made a more valuable recruit to the service than a first in Greek or Latin. But the Committee's onslaught on the cult of the generalist tended in that direction.

There are, of course, two different ideas and I confess that I frequently confuse them. No undergraduate degree makes a man or woman a specialist. It simply registers a certain level of tested ability at a certain age. Here I am clear that the civil service should continue to recruit the best talent available, casting its net wide. The question of specialized skills is another matter and, by implication, I have already conceded the need for it.

I do not doubt that the civil service requires economic, financial and accountancy skills. I do not take a theological view of whether newish recruits to the service, especially the younger ones, should receive such training or whether the recruitment of men and women already skilled makes more sense — this is something for those far more experienced in recruitment and training than I am. But as a Minister faced with the need for advice and some understanding of the political and governmental process, generalist ability — and a capacity to learn — is what I require in the officials who surround me.

Two other quick thoughts arising from Fulton. First, I am inclined to think that seniority is still too large a factor in promotion. If a man or woman can join the Cabinet before the age of 40 or be a Vice-

21

Chancellor or a captain of industry or the government's chief economic adviser, there is no obvious reason why he cannot be a Permanent Secretary.

Second, while I have no experience of the Civil Service College, I am inherently sceptical about institutional arrangements that help to preserve the segregation of the civil service. I would like to see as much training as possible carried out in open educational establishments. I would welcome an obligatory sabbatical year for every high flyer probably around the age of 40 and certainly before promotion to Under-Secretary.

I have been speaking tonight in an entirely personal way about my experience of Westminster and Whitehall. I am more than ready to be persuaded that I have got it wrong, perhaps through omission or even a misunderstanding of essentials. Strong views can be held either way on a number of the issues I have mentioned. I expect that some of my colleagues in government would disagree profoundly with what I have said.

But after almost eighteen years in the House of Commons, more than half of them spent in government, I am very sure of one point and quite immovable on it: the need to maintain the primacy of Parliament. The organization of Whitehall *can* be improved; the Civil Service *can* adapt the change, we *can* have more Ministers and more departments — or fewer. But Ministers must continue to answer to Parliament, prevent the erosion of its powers, and respect the authority that is vested in those elected to serve there.

At the end of a hard day, a Minister may find it wearing to remain at the House of Commons until after 10 o'clock, or even much later. Similarly, it is tempting for a Minister to aspire to be chairman of the board, running a big business like any other. But he is not. He is a Member of Parliament, fortunate to have additional responsibilities for the time being. He should never forget it.

Discussion

Elaborating on the need for MPs to have some kind of training to give them a better understanding of Whitehall, Mr. Rodgers said that when he became a junior Minister in the old Department of Economic Affairs — after only two-and-a-half years in Parliament — he had never previously been in a Whitehall department. He commented that it was strange that MPs did not normally talk to civil servants rather than to Ministers. As a Minister he had himself been "wary" if told that an opposition spokesman wanted to talk to one of his officials, but in practice he felt that "We're much too stuffy about that.... It ought to be possible for MPs actually to go and talk frankly to civil servants — not about matters of high policy and controversy but to do it much more naturally and normally than is now the case."

Asked about the proper division of responsibilities between Ministers and civil servants, Mr. Rodgers said that Ministers were already very busy and heavily burdened. His first principle was that Ministers should not be given any more responsibilities of a detailed kind "which will divert them from their main job of policy making in the fullest sense." Secondly, though Ministers did rightly have a say in choosing people to work in their Private Offices and as Permanent Secretaries and other senior officials in their own departments, they should not become involved in the details of promotion policy, in expressing detailed views about individual officials, or in "manpower budgeting", for example in such questions as the number and grades of staff in the Department of Transport's Railways Division. On all these matters Ministers could not hope to be more sophisticated or competent than their Permanent Secretaries, whom they must trust. "If they don't trust their Permanent Secretaries they should seek to change them." For related reasons it was wrong to consider the big departments created in the late 1960s and early 1970s as better because they were bigger, and to talk about "line management which involved the Minister. I don't think it works that way. One consequence of the biggest conglomerate departments of that time was to take Ministers away from Parliament and to make Parliament much less effective in helping to determine policy."

Asked about the difference between officials' contact with the public and with the parliamentary process, Mr. Rodgers said that most civil servants knew what was going on in the world around them. But they were very shy and cautious towards Parliament, as a result of the tradition that the career civil servant should be seen to be non-party political. "Civil servants spend a great deal of time essentially with other civil servants — dining with them and lunching with them — and it may be it's because they are afraid somehow of talking shop outside the shop because they are going to give away secrets...". Somehow this problem had to be overcome; there had to be a great deal more frankness, and a recognition that politics was a tough process. Civil servants were probably too fastidious about that. "They like the whole panoply of government but they don't somehow like the thought that down beneath it there are some unpleasant things going on. And that's why most civil servants would like a very broad coalition of all the parties: because instinctively they're Whigs, they believe the power of reason should triumph and if all good men and true of moderate opinions got together, everything would be fine." He then went on to tell how he had taken two of his Private Secretaries to his constituency to visit his own constituency surgery.

23

Mr. Rodgers was asked about the value to him, as a Minister, of policy advisers. He said that the experience of different Ministers probably differed here. Not long before he became a Secretary of State he had had great doubts about having a Special Adviser, partly because he knew from previous experience that it was always possible to recruit experts as necessary from outside, partly because as a politician he felt that he did not need advice on the political aspects of his job, or on the correct interpretation of the party manifesto. But in the first place, Ministers had to get through a great deal of work; and, secondly, the Private Office's job was simply to ensure that the papers came into Ministers in the right way and that the department and the Minister were adequately explained to each other. A good Private Office serving a busy Minister would be worked extremely hard and would not have the time to think in depth about particular issues. He had come to feel that he needed another pair of hands. In theory this would not be hard to get if it was all that a Minister wanted. When as Secretary of State for Transport he had first met his Permanent Secretary he had made the point that although he was Secretary of State for Transport "in the fullest way I want[ed] to be a Member of Cabinet and I want[ed] to go to Cabinet as well briefed as a Treasury Minister.... A unit was set up for trying to brief me for Cabinet but it was very hard work indeed, because the range of issues coming before Cabinet is large, and the people who were briefing me, although they were very good, had other responsibilities as well." That arrangement had not worked well. It had been hard to find people available within the Department with the necessary qualities — which included intelligence and a high level of political perception. Additionally, any Minister ought to try and have a wide range of contacts with people outside his department, Parliament and his constituency.

A Special Adviser was a great help here, acting as another pair of eyes and ears. People would often tell him that they had not been able to contact him but had contacted his Special Adviser. The aim was not to subvert his professional advisers but to help bring another dimension to his thinking. Sometimes the Special Adviser's contribution was "political", in the sense of bringing some quality of the outside world into departmental thinking. But in general, the Special Adviser advised on matters going to Cabinet not in terms of their political dimension but because he could see behind some issues and put his finger on the central matter to be discussed.

Whether this arrangement worked depended on the Special Advisers themselves, Ministers and officials. But it was essential that there should be nothing which a Special Adviser told the Minister which the Minister could not tell the Private Secretary — so not to undermine his relationship with the latter. Although the arrangement had worked well for Mr. Rodgers personally, it had not done so for all of his colleagues or in all departments. But in general the principle of Special Advisers seemed likely to take root and Whitehall should adapt itself accordingly.

Collective Responsibility: Fact, Fiction or Façade?

EDMUND DELL

It is sometimes claimed for the British Constitution that the fact that it just grew gives it a flexibility which written constitutions lack. Closer examination of its actual workings reveals, however, that it is most flexible where flexibility is least desirable — in the degree of protection which it affords to human rights — at least flexible where flexibility is more desirable — in the system of government itself.

Certainly flexibility is a difficult operational requirement to write into constitutions. Some states have achieved the necessary flexibility by revolution, others have attempted to do so by re-interpreting or amending their written constitutions. United Kingdom experience shows that tradition can entrench inflexibility as surely as can the written words of a constitution. It does so by creating constitutional conventions which guide and constrain behaviour long after any rational basis for them has gone. One such convention is collective responsibility.

To criticize the doctrine of collective responsibility is not to question the need for collective discussion of major issues in Cabinet or Cabinet Committees. It does not question the frequent need for collective decision-making where decisions involve more than one department, though collective responsibility does make for an excess of collective decision-making because of an understandable insistence by those who are to be responsible to share in the decision making. It is not to deny that a government should have a collective purpose, whether pragmatic or philosophical, identifying the intended road ahead. Finally, critics of collective responsibility must accept the need within a government for collective tolerance; that is, that Ministers should not set out to undermine their colleagues' positions and policies if they can possibly bring themselves to avoid it.

But collective responsibility is different from collective discussion, collective decision-making, collective purpose or collective tolerance. The emphasis is on the word responsibility. It is collective *responsibility* that creates the political absurdities and administrative complexities. To summarize the argument of this lecture, collective responsibility has no clear meaning but that does not prevent its being invoked as a discipline and imposing excessive demands on Ministers. It is

27

counter-productive politically, and attempts to meet its requirements are cumbersome administratively. But it is not enough to get rid of it. It is necessary also to enhance the central position of the Prime Minister, something which with all its dangers I believe necessary to good government in this country. My conclusion will be that within the compass of the parliamentary system we need a rather more presidential form of prime ministerial government, less dependent on collective consent and not at all on collective responsibility.

I will start by discussing the political consequences of the doctrine of collective responsibility. I do not wish to claim that the machinery of government in general, or collective responsibility in particular, are at the root of this country's recent political and economic failures. These have been due to failures of energy, of will and of foresight, not of the machinery of government. However, it is of the nature of collective responsibility that it should continually enforce the substitution of policies decided by Cabinet consensus (how can I get my Cabinet colleagues to agree?) for policies decided on merit (what if anything should I do?).

The propagation of myths has sometimes been claimed to be an essential feature of successful government. They serve to hold societies together. Of the myth of collective responsibility it is claimed that it serves to hold governments together. However, for a myth to perform this useful service it is necessary that it be believed, and belief is the essential ingredient which this particular myth now lacks. Gibbon wrote that: "The various modes of worship which prevailed in the Roman world were all considered by the people as equally true, by the philosopher as equally false, and by the magistrate as equally useful". Thus the magistrates found the myths useful because the people found them true.

Collective responsibility is a myth and one which is not believed. Let us examine a few definitions and see what assent they would command. The first of these definitions could be that all Ministers must agree on all decisions of government. This requirement would simply be preposterous. A second definition might be that all Ministers must be equally responsible for all decisions of government. No one, not even the House of Commons, would believe this to be true or necessary. The House of Commons censures, or attempts to censure, particular Ministers. Rightly, it holds particular Ministers to be questionable in respect of any default. Many Ministers, including Cabinet Ministers, are ignorant of many of the decisions of government up to the time they are announced. Some decisions of government which are not announced remain unknown to many members of the Government, including Cabinet Ministers. To be *collectively* (as against *departmentally*) responsible for a decision of which you are ignorant is a refinement of constitutional mythology, impossible even for the

IGNORANCE OF MANY DECISIONS

28

British Constitution.

A third definition might require that whereas all Ministers cannot be equally responsible for all decisions of government, they must at any rate be bound by all decisions of government. To be bound simply to silence, to conceal one's dissent from the world while being held collectively responsible, is a form of punishment which in recent practice and in cases of importance, few Ministers have been ready to accept. Indeed, a principal incentive to leakages from Cabinet is the fear of a Minister that he might otherwise be held to concur with decisions for which he is not in fact prepared to accept responsibility. Collective responsibility is therefore a myth, a myth in which no one believes and a myth whose various definitions range from the preposterous to the counter-productive. Can it really be true that good government in this country can depend in any significant degree on such a myth?

There is, however, another definition of collective responsibility which perhaps comes nearer to what the public these days actually expect from Ministers. This definition is that Ministers are collectively responsible by the simple fact of not have resigned. They may disagree with the decisions, and even deny personal responsibility for them, but at any rate they do not find it intolerable to remain in a government which has made them. They provide a cover for such decisions by their continuing presence in government.

In fact, however, collective responsibility is taken to imply very much more than that, even though these days the obvious inconsistencies between the theory and the practice make it difficult to provide any clear definition. The absence of any clear definition may suggest impending demise. But it is not dead yet. It rallies to cause confusion whenever the difficulties are greatest. As such it is an impediment to good and efficient government. It is less of an impediment after a successful election result when the prestige of victory endows a vigorous Prime Minister with the means of forcing recalcitrant colleagues into line. It is more of an impediment when difficulties accumulate and the Cabinet demands and obtains more influence over the course of government policy, thus causing delay and exposing indecision.

This is the precise opposite of what ideally collective responsibility at its best should provide. Prime Ministers are not always wise in the aftermath of a successful election result. They may think that endorsement by the electorate proves the rightness of the often oversimplified policies on which they were elected. It is then, rather than later, that they need the guidance of any wise colleagues they are fortunate enough to have, and it is precisely then that they are least susceptible to the disciplines of collective responsibility.

In government, as in other walks of life, decisions have to be made.

Sometimes they have to be made quickly. The decisions then made will probably correspond to the wishes of the Prime Minister or to those of the Minister directly responsible, if he is strong enough, or to those of an explicit majority of the Cabinet. In all normal circumstances, if a Prime Minister has made up his mind about an issue, he will get his way. Indeed most of the Cabinet will be delighted to relinquish to him their collective responsibility for issues with which they have no direct concern. They will like nothing better than to have a strong Prime Minister taking a strong lead in a successful government. They know the Prime Minister will take most of the credit when things go well and they will have no objection at all to his taking most of the blame when they start going badly. There will, however, be dissentients who will resent his dominance, will disagree with his policies and will wish to argue their case in Cabinet.

There is at least some consolation in having stated one's case even if one's argument does not prevail. One may later be able to say: "I told you so". There is indeed an undeniable right to state one's case even on matters far beyond one's departmental responsibilities if one is to be held at the end collectively responsible for the decision. One may bore the Cabinet by persisting in advocating lost causes, but to do so is an undoubted right.

Prime Ministers therefore have to accept the risk and tedium of listening to their colleagues. But then so do their colleagues. The reaction of Prime Ministers to the tedia of Cabinet government is to retreat into an inner Cabinet. This works if the Prime Minister is strong, determined and knows what he wants. Otherwise the meeting of the inner Cabinet is merely a preparation for further squabbles in Cabinet. It can thus consume more time instead of saving time. There is in fact no way of avoiding loss of time other than for the Prime Minister to act as though collective responsibility does not exist. He will then make his major decisions with the assistance only of those colleagues most intimately involved and leave the others to protest if they dare. It is an oddity of collective responsibility that often the major decisions other than on public expenditure are made without regard to it and that it is then mainly the lesser decisions that fall victim to its cumbersome processes.

This is certainly the way governments tend to work when they are successful and in their early days. The test comes when there are serious difficulties and when therefore Ministers clamour to be involved. I take as an example the economic crisis in the autumn of 1976. So much has been written and leaked about those weeks that I am probably guilty of an excess of propriety in not adding my own mite to the revelations. Rather, I draw some conclusions from what is already known. They are not, I think, favourable to the reputation of collective responsibility.

Because the decisions then to be made concerned cuts in the level of public expenditure, the whole Cabinet had to be involved. Because no spending Minister could allow his budget to be cut without a struggle, there had to be a long debate in Cabinet meeting after Cabinet meeting, virtually in public view. The public was entertained by a series of leaks favourable to the spending Ministers. After all, spending Ministers had to demonstrate to a possibly sceptical public how hard, even if unsuccessfully, they were fighting. The battle against spending cuts demanded its own individual economic analysis. Ministers who prized their reputation as economists, who doubted the economic validity of the arguments leading to the spending cuts, and in any case saw little substance in social democracy if it did not involve high public spending, also had to make it publicly known how bitterly they were fighting against economic illiteracy and the powers of darkness represented by Denis Healey and the IMF. To their friends in the press they had to make it clear that they were winning the argument even if nothing else. After all it was most unreasonable of the IMF to lend money only on conditions. Did the IMF not know that we had a natural right to be saved from the consequences of our own actions with their money but without their conditions?

In retrospect, it is quite clear that this public spectacle of a Cabinet in travail was a farce, and a dangerous farce at that. Either the Cabinet would have to concede substantially to Denis Healey's proposals or it would collapse. It had no intention of collapsing and therefore it had to concede. The only question was for how long, in a situation of economic crisis, it could affaord to act out the farce. Once the Prime Minister had decided that enough was enough and that he had to make clear his support for the Chancellor of the Exchequer, that was the end of the matter.

The Prime Minister's dilemma was purely tactical. There was never at any time any question but that he would support the Chancellor of the Exchequer. There was therefore at no time any question but that the Cabinet as a whole would submit to the Chancellor of the Exchequer. The Prime Minister could have taken the tactical decision to avoid the damaging farce and force the Cabinet to come to a conclusion rapidly, perhaps even at one meeting. Or, fearing resignations, he could allow Cabinet Ministers time to talk themselves out. That would not perhaps be good for the reputation of the Government; it would be taking risks with the market, but it would allow dissident Ministers to put on a good show and then retire from the battlefield with both honour and their Cabinet positions intact. The main danger in such a long-playing tactic is that Ministers will paint themselves into a corner, but most are too skilled to engage in such self-destructive folly.

Under conditions of collective responsibility one cannot blame a Prime Minister who judges it tactically wiser to permit his Ministers sufficient time to display their histrionic talents before they accept the inevitable. One must also think of the reaction of the parliamentary party to too rapid a submission to the IMF. But it would be difficult to claim that this is a sensible system of government. A system of government is tested not by its moments of success but by its moments of crisis. At a moment of crisis, collective responsibility is a recipe for delay, deliberate indiscretions, histrionics and eventually humiliation. Better let the Prime Minister take the decision upon his shoulders with such consultations with the Cabinet and with particular Ministers as he judges wise in the circumstances.

PENDING

One of the advantages of replacing collective responsibility by collective purpose could be that it would remove public expenditure from the arena of collective decision-making. Public expenditure decisions inevitably divide Treasury Ministers from their colleagues in charge of the great spending departments. It is absurd that decisions about the level of public expenditure should be arrived at by compromise between the Chancellor of the Exchequer on the one hand and the spending Ministers on the other. The level of public expenditure is an issue central to the responsibilities of the Chancellor of the Exchequer. He should be as free in determining that level as he should be in proposing to Parliament in his budget what should be done on the revenue side. In fact his freedom on the revenue side is constrained by public expenditure decisions taken in Cabinet by the usual process of horse-trading and compromise. The Chancellor of the Exchequer may decide that for economic reasons he wishes to increase his budget deficit. But he should not be pushed into such a decision by his lack of control over the level of public expenditure combined with his apprehensions about the political effects of increasing the levels of taxation. It is inevitable that there will be political constraints on the actions of a Chancellor of the Exchequer. His task should not be made impossible by the compromise forced on him through the operations of collective responsibility.

Spending Ministers may claim that the level of public expenditure is as central to their responsibilities as it is to those of the Chancellor of the Exchequer. Such a claim should not be allowed. Certainly they must be consulted on the question of need. But the determining factor must be a judgment as to the availability of resources which the Chancellor of the Exchequer should be responsible for making and for which he should need the support only of the Prime Minister. Economic responsibility would thus be clearly located where it should be, on the Prime Minister and the Chancellor of the Exchequer. Spending Ministers have the responsibility only of deploying to the

PM & CHANCH· TO MAKE SPENDING LEVELS

32

best effect the resources which government can make available to them. Equally, however, spending Ministers should not be expected to take public responsibility for the level of resources at their disposal. If they feel them to be so grossly inadequate as to make their job impossible, they will of course resign. Otherwise they will get on with their real task of deciding priorities within their departmental budget. On the principle of collective tolerance they will avoid making speeches denouncing the Chancellor of the Exchequer. But the position will be perfectly well understood.

[margin note: SHOULD THEY RESIGN? BE REPLACE BY OPPONENTS]

The relationship, which, politically, is most inconsistent with collective responsibility is that between a Minister and his closest associates in the parliamentary party. It is through such relationships that the unity of government and parliamentary party is preserved if at all. A Minister who has any independent political substance will have links with backbench MPs who will regard him as their man or as one of their men in Cabinet. They will want to know from him what is going on. They will expect him to argue his and their point of view. They will not want him to surrender his dissident view to the Prime Minister or to the majority of the Cabinet. They will expect him to be responsive to their representations. But they will not, in most circumstances, want him to resign. They will understand that there are limits to what he can achieve and to what he can tell them. They will be the more understanding the more frank he finds it possible to be.

Ministers thrive not just on their ability but on their contacts, particularly in the parliamentary party. It is not possible for an ambitious Minister to cut himself off from his political friends just because he is in the government and they are not. Nor, from the point of view of the government, is it even desirable. To the degree that he is frank, he is dependent on the discretion of his friends. It will be remarkable if a great deal is not revealed publicly through such contacts and through the contacts his backbench friends have with political journalists, even if the Minister is not himself giving the whole game away more directly. But unless he is sufficiently frank, he will not be able to perform his function, an important function in our system of parliamentary government, of maintaining the general support for the government of his friends in the House of Commons. He performs that function not by pretending to share responsibility for decisions with which he disagrees but by exercising his influence both in Cabinet and in the parliamentary party and by acting as a link between the two. In the end he will resign only if he is so totally out of sympathy with the government's course of action that life with colleagues has become intolerable; in other words if the decisions being made lie outside the bounds of collective tolerance.

Collective responsibility is an enemy of open government. Open government requires that real options should be presented, whether in Green Papers or otherwise, and publicly debated. It is inevitable that responsible Ministers should become associated with one or other of the real options available. After all it is to be assumed that all the options are consistent with the collective purpose of the government, and therefore it would be entirely permissible for a Minister to prefer one option rather than another. It is nonsense to require that after public debate Ministers should surrender their own point of view because they have not carried a majority in Cabinet, or that they should be forced under questioning to use circumlocutory language to conceal their actual dissent from the Cabinet decision. They do not need to undermine what the Cabinet has decided. But equally they should not be made to suffer the humiliation of apostasy in the name of collective responsibility, a humiliation from which they are protected only by the sensible acceptance by the public that there are bound to be differences between Ministers.

The more open government becomes, the more genuine debate there is about the real options in formulating policy, the more incompatible with open government will the doctrine of collective responsibility be seen to be. By the same token, those who fight most vigorously for collective responsibility will be least inclined to public debate of real options. I would add that if public debate leads a government to a conclusion on some important matter inconsistent with the views of the Minister directly responsible, he should resign or be moved. These days Ministers seldom resign, partly no doubt because resignation is dangerous to ambition, but partly also because they consider themselves not so much departmental Ministers as emanations of a political force designated for the moment to manage a particular department on behalf of that force. If the political force decides some matter of departmental importance against their better judgment, then within the present concept of collective responsibility they can easily persuade themselves to regard their responsibility to their collectivity as over-riding their responsibility as departmental Ministers. On no Minister should the onus be put of carrying through a policy of importance with which he fundamentally disagrees. It is one of the costs of collective responsibility that precisely that can happen and that the doctrine can be used as an excuse by such a Minister for staying in post.

It was a practice in the Labour Government where broad perspectives were under review, such as the direction of the Government or our relations with Europe or our proposals for devolution, to have all-day Cabinets sometimes at Chequers at which every Cabinet Minister could deliver himself of such thoughts as he had accumulated either within his own head or from those of his officials. These were pleasant enough occasions. They made a nice break from work.

Occasionally they served to suppress incipient revolts such as on devolution by showing up how much fight there actually was in the dissidents. They may have brought some satisfaction to those Ministers for whom it was more important to have registered a view than to have persuaded colleagues. But as time passed it became clear, I think, that busy Ministers increasingly resented the time devoted to them. This may be a criticism of Ministers whose horizons were increasingly narrowed by departmental responsibilities. But perhaps it is far more a criticism of a system of government which plunges Ministers into Cabinet after Cabinet, Cabinet Committee after Cabinet Committee, and hence into a mountain of detail concerning matters outside their departmental responsibilities, thus consuming such intellectual energies as some few of them might otherwise devote to defining wider horizons.

It is customary to blame the civil service for exhausting Ministers with detail. One could indeed understand it if civil servants considered some Ministers as being more innocently engaged on their departmental affairs, under some sort of departmental guidance, than in Cabinet speculating at large about the future. But the truth is, as in so many matters for which the civil service is blamed, that it is the fault of Ministers if they tamely submit to the burdens forced upon them by the doctrine of collective responsibility.

Among the more amusing moments in any Cabinet meeting are those when a Prime Minister complains about leaks. It will, he will say, do the government no good at all that it should be known that there are differences between Ministers. The Prime Minister will not accuse anyone specifically, but suspicion will tend to fall on the losers because it will be thought, not always correctly, that it is they who have the strongest motive to leak. The amusement among Cabinet Ministers will, however, be at its height when it is suspected that the leak has in fact come from No. 10 Downing Street itself, probably with the full authority of the Prime Minister, who wishes thereby to pass a message to one or more of his colleagues that he is not entirely content with them.

It may be thought that the polite fictions of collective responsibility are a small price to pay for the cohesion it lends to a government. Collective responsibility may have been harmless enough in the nineteenth century when the range of government concerns was much less. It may indeed have been a necessary instrument for holding governments together at a time when the party system was less strong. One can understand Melbourne pleading with his Cabinet that if they did not hang together they would hang separately. Today the cohesion of governments does not, and indeed could not, depend on collective responsibility.

It depends rather on the party system and on the width of policy differences from the Opposition. In fact it is easily observable over a long period of political history that collective responsibility helps least when difficulties are greatest. It is then that the leaks proliferate, that Ministers try to defend their separate points of view with elements of outside opinion, that the whole concept of collective responsibility becomes more and more ragged, and when indeed Prime Ministers appeal to their colleagues, with ever-increasing desperation, not to leak, not to give the government an appearance of disunity — to think if they can think of nothing else, of the effect of their leaks on the future prospects of the government, prospects upon which they depend more for their own political futures than they do upon conciliating personally some friendly spectrum of opinion. But it does not work. Governments crumble according to laws of their own, and among the most efficient under-miners are dissident Ministers making their semi-private self-exculpations from the burden of collective responsibility.

The supposed benefits of collective responsibility therefore no longer exist. We are left with its costs. It wastes time. It confuses real responsibility. It blunts decision making with ill thought-out compromises.

Politically, therefore, collective responsibility may fairly be described as counter-productive. It is also an inefficient way of running a government. The range of work undertaken by a modern government is very wide. The breadth of a government's concerns, and the amount of business conducted, have combined with the requirements of collective responsibility to lead to the formation of a multitude of Cabinet Committees which take decisions on behalf of the Cabinet. As one effect of collective responsibility is to push all decisions upwards, far too many decisions have to be made in Cabinet Committees. Normally these decisions are taken as decisions of the government as a whole and are not even reported to the Cabinet. Some decisions taken in Cabinet Committees are more important than most decisions taken in Cabinet. There may be an appeal to the Cabinet when important differences of opinion emerge in a Cabinet Committee. The criteria governing such appeals are laid down by the Prime Minister. The Prime Minister will usually be reluctant to allow an appeal except on a very important question or when a very strong Minister is demanding it, for fear of cluttering the Cabinet agenda. Sometimes the Prime Minister will call a subject in from a Cabinet Committee if he disagrees with the decision, or if he thinks the issue of major political importance. Sometimes, in such a case, he will have decided to chair the Cabinet Committee himself and the decision then will almost invariably be final. The decision-making process will thus have little appearance of collective responsibility. It all illustrates how the scope of modern government has made collective responsibility a practical impossibility.

Within these Committees an attempt will be made by discussion to formulate policies for which all its members, and hopefully all the government, can feel collectively responsible. Possibly a parallel committee of officials will already have sought and failed to find such a solution. There will usually be one particular Minister who has the lead and who has clear personal responsibility. He will be in the position, quite often, of having to modify his preferred view to meet the objections of colleagues. There can be great value in collective discussion. A Minister who has to defend his policy to an audience of critical colleagues will prepare his case and his conclusion all the better for it. Difficulties arise because they have to share his responsibility. Because they share his responsibility they are more insistent and he is forced to make more concessions to their views even against his better judgment. Clear decision-making is compromised and real responsibility is confused.

Ministers are human and over-burdened. Cabinet Committees can be very time-consuming. Because of the burdens Ministers carry, including the burden of frequent attendance at Cabinet Committees, they may not have had time to study their colleagues' papers properly. They may have received them only the previous evening and may have had time merely to skip through them, possibly after midnight. They may not have thought very deeply about the subject matter and may not have much background of personal experience to help them decide whether what is proposed is sensible or not. They hear a discussion in which a Minister who is a close friend and political associate is embattled against other ministerial colleagues less close in personal terms and political view-point. Naturally they support their friends, not out of conviction but out of loyalty. The Committee may split between trends of opinion based on past or present political loyalties which have nothing at all to do with the matter in hand. The result may be not just compromises, but compromises forced by ignorance on knowledge.

[handwritten margin note: DO THEY ALWAYS? WETS REFUSED TO REVOLT IN '81 OVER BUDGET]

Decisions taken in such Committees are likely on the whole to be less good than if they were taken by the lead Minister himself in consultation with his colleagues rather than collectively with his colleagues. It is after all that Minister who will have considered the matter most carefully before bringing his views to his colleagues. Where more than one department will be significantly affected by a decision, it must be taken jointly and agreed between all the Ministers directly concerned. But there again it is much better to strive towards agreement forged between Ministers who know the subject, and then discuss it with a few colleagues if it is of any importance, than to have decisions influenced by extraneous considerations and by colleagues ignorant of the subject matter.

37

If the Ministers primarily concerned can agree, well and good. If they cannot agree, the Prime Minister will have either to involve himself or find some other way of forcing a decision. But almost anything is better than permitting arbitration by a collection of Ministers uninterested in the subject matter and uninvolved in any real responsibility for the result.

Collective responsibility confers upon every Minister an equal right to be awkward, even ignorantly awkward. Exploitation of this right is a particular temptation to those whose approach to political decision-making is ideological rather than pragmatic. Indeed one can find cases in which an ideological Minister who has succumbed to pragmatism within his own department will nevertheless attempt to deny to colleagues the benefit of the very pragmatism he has adopted for himself. Nothing is more worrying to an ideological Minister turned pragmatist than another colleague who is also attempting to decide issues on their merits.

Another situation in which this right to be awkward created by collective responsibility is exploited is where Ministers argue that "We have to be politicians, not simply administrators." Speaking generally, the Minister directly responsible is more likely to decide a question on merit than Ministers whose interest is marginal. There is perhaps little harm in being "politicians" when what is proposed is to implement a settled collective purpose. Too often, this ambition to be a politician simply describes a wish to agree with one's friends, perhaps in some significant interest group, or the desire to relieve some industrial problem in a marginal constituency, or more generally to inject into the discussion some calculations of political advantage. Collective responsibility enables responsible Ministers to be pushed in that direction. I doubt whether these calculations of political advantage are often correct. Governments, however, are certainly afraid that the opposition of an articulate and well organized minority can involve political costs greater than the political benefits to be gained by appearing sensible and incorruptible. Collective responsibility can too easily divert a discussion on merits to a discussion on politics — a type of discussion which does not have to be informed by a careful prior consideration of the papers actually under discussion. Given the diseconomies of the processes of collective responsibility, it it perhaps surprising that governments do as well as they do.

It may be thought that collective responsibility is justified as being the only known way of persuading a Minister actually to read a paper put in by one of his colleagues. If he is not to be responsible for what is decided, why should he read it? This indeed may be the most persuasive argument for collective responsibility. I reject it on the pragmatic ground that I have discovered that a sense of collective responsibility does not in fact suffuse Ministers, and does not lead them to read papers, and that the Ministers who seem to be the most bowed down by their respectable adherence to this ancient myth are those typically who, not having read the papers, maintain a prudent silence. The more vigorous contestants in any discussion are not likely to feel collectively responsible if they disagree with the conclusion, and are motivated to study simply by their desire to move the government in one direction rather than another.

The principal administrative objection to collective responsibility is that it confuses responsibility. To make everyone responsible means in the end that no one feels responsible. Responsible government depends to a very high degree on the personal standards and self-discipline of departmental Ministers and of officials individually. Even the most responsible Minister will find it difficult enough to impose upon himself the standards of judgment that he would bring to a comparable decision if he were in the private sector and real money, not government money, were at stake. Of course government money should be real money and should be regarded as such by no one more than by a Minister. It is only too clear in governments of all parties that decisions involving government money are taken more lightly than they should be in the conviction that there is no identifiable owner and that there is more to come whence it came. Errors of judgment carry fewer penalties because the problems they create can be swamped by further doses of public money. It is in fact already difficult for the most responsible Minister to be as careful as he should be. The temptations of interventionism and the pressures for it are so great. To allow him the easy escape of collective responsibility or to over-rule him and thereby to force upon him policies with which he does not agree or compromises that he accepts only unwillingly is to threaten the foundations of responsible public policy.

It may be thought that the machinery of collective responsibility will act as a constraint on profligate Ministers. This is very much a matter of chance. For example, Industry Ministers may through experience become sceptical of the efficacy of the policy instruments available to them. They may see some role for interventionism, but not the somewhat exaggerated role drawn by political propaganda. I have seen Industry Ministers pressed into expenditure by their colleagues at least as frequently as I have seen them constrained by their colleagues. If press reports are to be believed, the Chrysler case was an example of this. But in any case the constraint on profligacy should not depend on the chance workings of collective responsibility, but on the strength of Treasury Ministers supported, as usually they should be, by the Prime Minister.

It may be feared that to end collective responsibility will simply enhance the power of the civil service. Ministers freed from the ideological pressure of their colleagues will fall even more rapidly than before under the influence of the officials. I cannot deny that this may happen but the fear of it brings to the fore another fault in our system of government: that it produces too many inadequate Ministers. I cannot rectify all faults with one remedy. We live under a system in which ministerial office is confined to Members of Parliament and, indeed, mainly to Members of the House of Commons. One of the penalties is that not all Ministers are particularly effective either in their departments or in discussion with their Cabinet colleagues. If, in this situation, I have to choose, I prefer a department to be run by senior civil servants rather than by the Cabinet or by a Cabinet Committee, neither of which are likely to have any very intimate knowledge of departmental affairs, acting vicariously through an inadequate Minister.

In two respects the substitution of collective purpose for collective responsibility might help to mitigate this problem. First, as I will argue, it should be accompanied by greater discretion for the Prime Minister, and that discretion could include the appointment of Ministers from outside the House of Commons, to whom nevertheless the House of Commons would allow audience. These days there are outside the House of Commons some people who carry more political credibility with significant sections of opinion than almost anyone inside the House of Commons. Secondly, collective responsibility implies adherence, or at least the pretence of adherence, to the ideology of the government party.

It would be easier for some outsiders not Members of Parliament to join the Cabinet, starting perhaps with responsibility for some of the more technical departments, if they did not thereby have to commit themselves ideologically. I must confess that the myth of collective responsibility is not the main political obstacle to so valuable a development. Rather is it the jealousy and inflexibility of the House of Commons which, contrary to the practice of many other parliamentary assemblies, will not allow a "stranger" to address it. As a beginning and as an experiment it would be sensible to allow the Prime Minister discretion to choose the Law Officers of the Crown from outside the House, but for the House to allow them a voice in it. Perhaps it would also be necessary to permit the television cameras in, in order to ensure decent behaviour to Ministers who might not understand the curious traditions of the House.

A case study may perhaps illustrate something of the complexity and character of collective decision-making under conditions of collective responsibility. The example I propose to examine is quite a simple one: the situation facing the Labour Government, and particularly myself as Secretary of State for Trade, after Lord Denning and the Court of Appeal upheld Freddie Laker's case against my predecessor on the matter of Skytrain. There were two possible courses of action open: to appeal to the House of Lords or not to appeal. The considerations involved in that decision are, fortunately, public or can be derived from published material. I can therefore bring them together here.

What considerations then would favour an appeal to the House of Lords? The first was undoubtedly inertia. The civil aviation policy, against part of which Laker was fighting, had been approved by the House of Commons after lengthy negotiations with interested parties. It had been accepted, albeit reluctantly, by the major British airlines and by the unions. Nobody could be certain of the effect on existing scheduled services of introducing Skytrain. Even the Civil Aviation Authority had only proposed an experiment. The unions in particular were by no means in love with Laker and might resent a decision not to appeal, especially as there was held to be a good chance of winning. Why undermine a compromise policy painfully worked out after months of negotiation and thereby prejudice relations with the unions, in an era of voluntary incomes policy, when the recourse of an appeal to the Lords remained? One can see that some Ministers might regard relations with the unions as being at that time of much greater importance than whether Skytrain should fly. Moreover, there was the crucial issue, left in some doubt by the Court of Appeal, of the extent of Crown prerogative. Even if we lost in the Lords, the noble judges would perhaps settle that.

What arguments were there on the other side with which to answer these weighty considerations? First, the effect of Skytrain on existing schedule services might well prove to have been exaggerated. The idea of Skytrain was very popular especially in view of the widely received opinion that civil aviation is a racket and that a little genuine competition would do a great deal of good. One would expect governments to be attracted by popularity, but it is not necessarily a decisive argument, and rightly so. Moreover, collective decision-makers are not necessarily enthused at the thought of a colleague gaining approval by overturning previous policy while he still has a choice. Another consideration was that we were in the midst of the difficult Bermuda II negotiations. We were trying to get a better deal in our civil aviation relations with the USA and for our pains were being accused by the Americans of being hostile to competition. To switch policies and endorse Laker would be a nice card to play against the USA which previously had refused to admit Skytrain. They would now be forced to admit it if they were not to drain all credibility from their consumerist propaganda, propaganda they love to use when they feel themselves competitive.

We can then envisage, with an accuracy at least comparable to that of journalists acting out ministerial roles in a television programme, the collective discussions leading up to the decision whether or not to appeal. Minister A says don't bother me with unnecessary problems. I do not want to think again about civil aviation policy unless I am forced to do so by losing in the Lords. B says he is very worried about Crown prerogative. C says that we must keep the unions happy and that trade union official Y, who is involved in this matter, is a key figure in deciding his union's position on incomes policy. D says that the White Paper on civil aviation policy was a first-class document, and E that we all know that the judges are always against Labour governments. Whether that means we should or should not appeal is left unclear. But F says that Skytrain is very popular, that we should at any rate follow the CAA in allowing an experiment, and that to unleash it now would be a shrewd tactical move in Bermuda II; whereas G says that a bit of competition in civil aviation would do a power of good. I should add that H to M are present, but have not read the papers. Some of these Ministers are not interested, but a few at least will be determined, once they have heard the issues argued, to take some stand. After all they are collectively responsible.

What is there to note about this particular piece of collective decision-making? Firstly, the relative importance of the three substantial issues — Crown prerogative, incomes policy and relations with the unions, and civil aviation policy, all of them very different in nature — is unagreed as far as it affects the decision whether or not to appeal. But Ministers are perfectly entitled to have different views on such a question. Secondly, the potential arbitrators between the principal contestants are the other Ministers present. But how likely are they to have addressed their minds in any depth to this one problem which is perhaps one item on a long agenda? The probability is that, if pressed, they will vote with their friends and not on the basis of an independent judgment. Thirdly, the Minister who will have to take public responsibility for the decision and who has probably considered the problems most carefully, is greatly outnumbered. Indeed, some junior Ministers may be present with instructions from their masters to vote one way or the other without having heard the arguments orally presented at all. Fourthly, all those present, and all those of the government not present, are supposed to be collectively responsible.

There is nothing very unusual about such a situation. The disagreements are legitimate and an attempt must be made among those principally involved to come to a collective decision. But, in my judgment, to add the complication of collective responsibility to the complexities inevitably present in collective decision-making, is a serious error. To start with, most of those present should be sent back to their offices. Those actually involved should try to agree, and if they succeed should present their agreement for collective discussion in a slightly larger group. If they cannot agree, it must be for the Prime Minister to find some means of achieving and enforcing a decision which derives from the merits of the argument rather than from the votes of the least involved members of a Cabinet Committee. In this particular case, the civil aviation arguments against appealing to the House of Lords prevailed. In my view that decision was right, but arriving at it was made more difficult by the factor of collective responsibility.

Collective responsibility is a convention of British government which tends to weaken the centre and to diffuse the responsibilities of departmental Ministers. What is needed in British government is a stronger centre, and hence a stronger central control on matters such as the level of public expenditure. This should be combined with clearer ministerial responsibility on those matters falling within the responsibility of a single department where the interests of other Ministers are marginal or simply political. It is right to consult and to listen to colleagues' views. It is wrong to permit a situation to develop in which no one is clearly responsible for anything.

There is understandable objection to increasing the power of the Prime Minister. It is not that the ending of collective responsibility in itself increases the power of the Prime Minister. After all it is Prime Ministers who, in an often vain attempt to discipline their colleagues, insist most vigorously on the doctrine of collective responsibility. It is rather that an end to collective responsibility will make it even more necessary to enhance the position of the Prime Minister as the ultimate authority on government policy; and of the centre in its relations with the departments.

Collective responsibility was invented when the Prime Minister was simply *primus inter pares*. Today this is far from being the case. The Prime Minister has enormous patronage. He leads a party which normally has a majority in Parliament and which, often too unthinkingly and too uncritically, will pass legislation offered to it by the Government. We have, it has been argued with much justice, a system in this country of elected dictatorships, personified in the Prime Minister.

Yet so far the whole trend of our times has been towards increasing the power of Prime Ministers ever further without that power being adequately counter-balanced either by strengthening the constituional controls on governments or by the openness of government, or by more open and tolerant debate within governments. Many influences are currently at work which will in practice further strengthen the position of Prime Ministers, not the least of which arise from the media's concentration on their activities and from the almost exclusive role which party leaders play at election time. Moreover it is becoming increasingly clear that effective operation within the European Community requires that the status of the Prime Minister be enhanced. Otherwise he may be at a loss, within the European Council, compared with colleagues who *are* in a position to commit

43

EUROPE &
PM'S
CENTRALITY
To THIS
UK RELAT-
IONSHIP

their governments. There are certain respects in which the power of a Prime Minister should be enhanced, notably as an exponent of British and European interests in the European Council, in the control of public expenditure, and in supporting departmental Ministers against the damaging compromises which tend to flow from the procedures of collective responsibility. The Prime Minister must act to strengthen the centre of government in its relations with departments at the periphery rather than to strengthen collective control by the Cabinet over all departments.

It may be thought that as the Prime Minister already commands great political power, to add to it would involve a cost greater than any likely benefit. I do not ignore such considerations. But the right way of dealing with problems or dangers arising from the excessive power of governments, of Prime Ministers, or of simple whipped majorities in the House of Commons, lie in the area of constitutional reform rather than in that of the system of government with which I am dealing here. Certainly collective responsibility is now no adequate protection. There would be advantage in finding some way of entrenching human rights even in this democratic country of long tradition. Electoral reform might increase the ability of Parliament to control governments. If an effective system of select committees were to be created — or if that which has been created proves effective — that too will limit the power of governments and hence of Prime Ministers. What I am arguing is not that the power of government should be increased (indeed I would argue for the reverse), but that in certain respects the power of Prime Ministers within governments should be increased. In any case collective responsibility, good or bad, has little influence on these matters.

An end to collective responsibility would mean that government could be more open, that Ministers could be freer in what they said, constrained only by collective purpose and collective tolerance. In one sense also Prime Ministers may actually find themselves more at risk because it will be less easy for them to hide behind collective Cabinet responsibility. For example, they will personally be inextricably identified particularly with economic policy and it will be rather more difficult for them to present the dismissal of a Chancellor of the Exchequer as an appropriate response to economic problems.

Does the strengthening of the centre require the establishment of a Prime Minister's Department? To establish such a department would change the balance of power between the Prime Minister and his Ministers to an extent that I would consider undesirable. It would also create further frictions which would reduce, not enhance, the efficiency of government. No Minister in his senses will deny to the Prime Minister the opportunity, if he wishes, to consult departmental officials. In the case of the Treasury and of the Civil Service Department the Prime Minister has by his own appointments as First Lord of the Treasury and Minister of the Civil Service the right of direct access to officials. But his access to departmental officials does not arise from some legal entitlement. No Minister either will attempt to deny to a Prime Minister such private consultation outside government as he wishes to undertake.

To establish an executive office of the Prime Minister would strike clean contrary to a characteristic of British government which distinguishes it from American government — namely that it places, and rightly places, executive power in the hands of Ministers, not those of a Prime Minister or President. The formation of a Prime Minister's Department would be a long step in that direction. There is already the Central Policy Review Staff which maintains a critical watch on departments, and which advises all Ministers, and not just the Prime Minister. The Prime Minister has also such personal access to the CPRS as a source of advice as he wishes to exercise. The CPRS has shown that it performs a useful role in reviewing for all Ministers the significance of what any particular Minister is proposing. Such a role will continue to be useful under a system devoted to consulting colleagues, rather than sharing responsibility with them, that I am here proposing. Moreover the Prime Minister will probably have his own political advisers at No. 10, and he has the guidance, particularly on matters of machinery and the conduct of meetings, provided by the Secretary to the Cabinet. There is no reason why with all this assistance the Prime Minister should be unable to perform effectively the role outlined to him here. There is no need for him in addition to start on a road which could only lead, at a considerable cost in the efficiency of government, to undermining the rock on which British government should be built, the rock of individual ministerial responsibility.

My conclusion, as I have already stated, is that within the compass of the parliamentary system we need a more presidential and less collective form of prime ministerial government. This would not be anything resembling the American system. The government would still be responsible to Parliament and dependent on the support of a majority in Parliament. Ministers would have their own real, and indeed more independent, responsibilities to Parliament.

There are risks in a more presidential form of government. Presidents can be naive and inexperienced. But the British parliamentary system should provide some safeguards. Prime Ministers have usually had many years' training through membership of Parliament and of the Cabinet. It is possible to get rid of them in mid-term without going the length of a threatened impeachment. They are surrounded by Ministers who may be men of independent political substance. Nevertheless one must admit that there are risks, though they are risks against which the present system of supposed collective responsibility may also provide inadequate protection in the heroic aftermath of a general election victory. Against these risks there stand the positive benefits of more effective government. My vote goes for taking the risk.

Discussion

Several people queried Mr. Dell's basic thesis. Questions were asked, in particular, about the relationship between possible abolition of the doctrine of collective ministerial responsibility and the responsibility of individual Ministers for their own departmental activities. Replying to these points, Mr. Dell said: "It is already regrettably a part of the spirit of ministerial responsibility that Ministers will appear in the House of Commons and say that they did not know that something was going on even in their own department and expect thereby to be excused. I would certainly not myself free a Minister of responsibility for what goes on in his own department because within his department, whether he knows or not, he is entitled to know. But I would certainly excuse him from responsibility — in the absence of knowledge — for what goes on in some other department or is decided by a Cabinet Committee of which he is not a member and in discussions in which he has played no part."

In answer to a further question about the probable effects of abolishing the doctrine of collective responsibility, Mr. Dell said that this would not of itself automatically increase the power of the Prime Minister. "Indeed, as we know, Prime Ministers spend a great deal of their time, in Cabinet and elsewhere, trying to use collective responsibility in order to maintain control of Cabinet.... If you get rid of collective responsibility you would have to increase the power of the Prime Minister — the person whose support above all a departmental Minister would need to carry a policy, sometimes against the collective judgment of his colleagues with whom he had discussed it." In other words, increasing the power of the Prime Minister would not be a consequence of abolishing collective responsibility, but a prerequisite. Another questioner asked whether a departmental Minister who had the support of the Prime Minister was entirely free to ignore his other colleagues' wishes. Mr. Dell suggested that where an issue was within the responsibility of a single Minister, he should certainly consult his colleagues, but if he could get the Prime Minister's support for his decision, he should carry his own policies forward even if his colleagues disagreed.

Mr. Dell denied that abolishing collective responsibility would make it more likely that Ministers would refuse to support unpopular decisions or would distance themselves from an unpopular government. Ministers already did certain things because they did not feel collectively responsible. "It is precisely this attempt to exculpate oneself with one's backbench colleagues in the House of Commons that takes place at the moment...." This tendency was inevitable under present arrangements. It was unrealistic to suppose that the doctrine of collective responsibility would in any way help governments to survive: a government following unpopular policies would be held together, if at all, by its wish to survive; the House of Commons, in voting, would support it for the same reason. His own proposals simply recognized this reality: "As KoKo once said, 'If that is the case, why not recognize it?'" Mr. Dell went on to comment that the majority party in the House of Commons was bound, from time to time, to vote together in support of the government even if its members disagreed with specific decisions. "It is an essential element in the parliamentary system that if governments are to survive, Members of Parliament will, from time to time, vote against their personal judgment on an issue in support of the government — and I don't think that that is any different for Ministers...." Moreover, collective responsibility was not only unrealistic politically, but had administratively cumbersome consequences; large numbers of people had to be consulted on every decision. The result of involving in major decisions so many people who had given little thought to the issues concerned was that many decisions were less good than they would otherwise have been.

Abolishing collective responsibility should have no implications for the individual responsibility of Ministers. Mr. Dell suggested that "The most important form of responsibility within a government is the responsibility of a Minister for the conduct of his own department.... That ... should be the foundation of government." But this principle was repeatedly confused by collective responsibility, which was used by Ministers as an excuse for acting in their own departments in ways at odds with their own judgment. "If a Minister is forced by collective decision-making processes to do something within a department with which he fundamentally disagrees, he should resign." Ministers appeared to believe that their responsibility to the collectivity was greater than their responsibility to their own departments. In fact, when the two types of responsibility were in conflict, individual ministerial responsibility should take precedence.

A questioner suggested that the essential value of collective responsibility was that it made possible compromises among Ministers and so allowed the development of a wide measure of support for public policies. The same questioner went on to suggest that Mr. Dell's view was a "managerial" one giving greater weight to the need to run a department efficiently than to the need to generate public support for policy. Mr. Dell commented that this view did not stand up to examination. Though he did not overlook the managerial element in a Minister's task, his approach was based not on managerial arguments but on political realism. "One of the problems in government are compromises inadequately worked out, ill-thought-out, arrived at in ways which no body of sensible people meeting together would really try and arrive at a conclusion on that particular subject." Discussions in a Cabinet Committee of, say, ten or twelve people were concerned with compromises rather than with establishing policy or merit. But the merit of a policy was the best way of maximizing support. It would be far better to have a Minister clearly publicly responsible for decisions with which he was known to agree. He cited one case in which a Minister "got up before the House of Commons and argued a case on a major issue, on the salvation of a particular company, which every single member of the House of Commons, indeed every informed person in this country, knew that he had opposed vigorously almost to the point of resignation.... But he thought ... that his responsibility to the collectivity was greater than his responsibility to his own judgment and his own department." Was this the way to develop consensus in the House of Commons and in the country?

Direct Rule in Practice

MERLYN REES

I kept typed diaries during my time as Shadow Spokesman and Secretary of State for Northern Ireland. Constantly, and particularly at the end of my period of office, I hear myself saying: the greater the length of time it is since one actually worked and lived in Northern Ireland, the greater is the chance of talking nonsense.

I have not lived there since the end of 1976. It is for this reason that I shall concentrate on my own experience in the past and will keep well away from the contemporary scene.

Between 1922 and March 1970 there was in Northern Ireland for the 1½ million people in the six counties a bicameral form of government, with a cabinet, a separate civil service, a judiciary, a privy council, and its own governor. The majority population in the North had not wanted its separate government. But by 1971 when I first became involved, and later, it was quite clear to me that the people wanted its own devolved government.

During the fifty years of its existence, the government in Northern Ireland had acted almost as if it were independent. Certainly Unionist Prime Ministers proceeded in that way, perhaps to match the existence of a Taoiseach in the South, and indeed kept industrial representatives in foreign states and sent Finance Ministers to international economic conferences.

In the context of my subject tonight this is by way of background to the Direct Rule of 1972.

During the period 1971 to 1974, when the power-sharing executive was formed and the Heath Government lost the general election, I spent a great deal of time in Northern Ireland. I found it impossible cost-wise to keep up the number and scale of the visits. The normal procedures of the House of Commons did not match the Irish situation and only an arrangement by Mr. Whitelaw whereby journeys could be "hitched" on the Ministers' planes travelling to and from Northern Ireland, together with the provision of transport within Northern Ireland on the grounds of security, made possible the continuation of my journeyings.

Something of this nature has continued since then for opposition spokesmen, for it is vital that the opposition spokesmen should visit the province frequently.

While it is not so true in recent years, between 1972 and 1974 the work within the House of Commons was very heavy and opposition spokesmen had to cope without the back-up of a government department. While this is normal for opposition spokesmen in general, it raised particular difficulties for those involved in Northern Irish affairs.

On the assumption of direct rule, which it was anticipated anyway would be short term, it was decided to keep the Northern Irish civil service in being.

I quote the words of Mr. Whitelaw early in his period as Secretary of State in the House of Commons:

> "I have also found in the last seven months that people in Northern Ireland expect in many aspects of administration a form of personal service which a remote United Kingdom authority in Westminster alone could not hope to provide. Equally, I have seen for myself that in spheres such as industrial development and industrial training, Northern Ireland administration, with its admirable Civil Service, has been able to meet special problems much more successfully by action on the spot than it would have if tied completely to arrangements applicable throughout the United Kingdom. It is also significant that such complete integration has very few advocates in Northern Ireland."

I echo those words.

At direct rule the old PM/Cabinet Office became the Northern Ireland Office. It consisted also of the existing Department of Home Affairs and its staff, together with UK civil servants, mainly then from the Home Office in London. The NIO concentrated on security, police, prisons, parliamentary matters and the constitutional settlement.

There was, in my view, a minimum of friction between the two civil services, though remember I was in opposition, despite some resentment of the "English" accents and of those who lived "in a luxury hotel". If only they had known! The facilities at the Culloden Hotel for a working office were poor. I was glad when in January 1975 we moved to the old Speaker's House at Stormont, with its offices and sleeping quarters. It is the best place for a Secretary of State to work from. I never stayed at Hillsborough as Secretary of State. Hillsborough is the place for a Governor, not a Secretary of State.

John Oliver has revealed, in his excellent book *Working at Stormont*, an initial problem with the English Private Secretaries to the junior Ministers who were responsible to the Secretary of State for the still existing Northern Irish Departments of Education, Agriculture, etc. These Private Secretaries travelled backwards and forwards with their Ministers but knew not Northern Ireland and its departments. This problem was corrected by, in effect, allowing the junior Ministers to keep their Westminster Private Secretaries and allowing a Northern Ireland Private Secretary to work to them from each department.

As Secretary of State — and it may well have been before, but I can only talk of my own experience — I met frequently with the civil service heads of the various departments and, of course, the head of the Northern Ireland civil service.

The Permanent Under-Secretary of the NIO also met weekly with his fellow PUSs and, given the responsibility of Ministers to Westminster for all aspects of government in Northern Ireland after the Macrory reforms in late 1972, this was vital.

It was clear that the Northern Irish civil servants had detailed knowledge of their province. It obviously was far greater than their counterparts in London could possibly have had of England and Wales. Given the responsibility for all the local government functions this knowledge was essential.

In such a small area, with a small population, it was not surprising that the civil servants knew each other socially. They had, perhaps, been to school together; they lived in the same area. The senior civil servants came from a different social background from most of their counterparts in England and Wales. Recruitment to the senior ranks of the civil service was, and still is, heavily weighted in favour of the majority community. Despite this, it is a service open to the talents. Promotion from the lowest grade, up the scale, was and is very common.

By its very nature, by its structure, the government of Northern Ireland has a tendency to lean towards the majority community. Despite all the changes that have been made under direct rule, any political head of the government there has to correct this list. Left to itself the Stormont rose bush goes back to its original briar.

In this respect I would emphasize the excellent relationships of the senior civil servants with the minority politicians who were the political heads of the various departments in the power-sharing executive, which tragically lasted for so short a time. Sadly, in May 1974 the Protestant working class with the full support of the Protestant community exercised their veto, just as the Provisional IRA and the minority community had exercised theirs in 1972.

I have no doubt, however, that the best way of governing Northern Ireland is to again involve both communities in government there.

The practice in Northern Ireland is that while the Secretary of State is responsible for all aspects of government, the junior Ministers are individually responsible for groups of individual departments.

Given its importance, the work of the Department of Commerce, which is responsible for industrial development, came into my ken more often than others of the local departments. The links between this Department and the industries of the province are close. It is just as well that the free market philosophy is not too strong there or industry would be in trouble.

The decline of the old staple industries and of the numbers in agriculture in Northern Ireland has been most marked. There has been an increase of firms in new engineering projects, etc. Nevertheless, the incidence of unemployment, particularly in certain areas of Belfast and particular towns, is still too high.

As far as industrial development is concerned I must give full praise to the work of the Northern Ireland Committee of Trade Unions and the Northern Ireland branch of the CBI. I saw a great deal of both of these bodies. They work positively together for the good of the province, both in and outside the Economic Planning Council.

The Department of Agriculture has close relationships with practising farmers. Its research facilities are second to none. The Department of Employment is heavily involved in economic planning and is not just a mirror of the UK department. It is because of the nature of local government and the area board system that I found the Department of Education is more closely involved with the schools than the department on this side of the water. The Department of Finance allows the switching of funds between the various departments of state in Northern Ireland. I found this an advantage when dealing with industrial projects. The problem of Treasury "control" in this respect is not as great as the one I noted when I became Home Secretary.

Before direct rule, however, there was no doubt in my mind that the weakest department was that of Home Affairs. Its long-term planning, its "control" of the RUC, was poor. There was far too much political control of the police. I took a conscious decision, as I feel sure did my predecessor, to free the police from political control. This does not mean that a Secretary of State should disengage from the RUC. Day-to-day involvement with the police in Northern Ireland does not mean political control. There was, and is, a need to help with obtaining the acceptance of the police by both communities. In this respect a developing role for the Police Authority is important.

It was a grave error of political judgment on all sides, and on both sides of the water, to have allowed the Special Powers Act to be on the Statute Book for so long. Any extraordinary powers such as were given in this Act need to have frequent discussion and approval. It was for this reason that an Emergency Provision Act for Northern Ireland is renewable every six months.

Of course, a government has the right and duty to deal with armed insurrection but I was right to stop the use of detention in 1975, as I was right to end the system of granting political status.

The responsibility for law and order is a major aspect of the work of a Secretary of State for Northern Ireland. The day-to-day involvement with the Chief Constable and the General Officer Commanding (GOC) in a war situation took up a large portion of the day.

There is one other aspect of the civil service in Northern Ireland that I would refer to: the relationship of Stormont MPs, Members of the Assembly and the Convention Members to the civil service in my period as Secretary of State for Northern Ireland. In the UK all relationships between elected representatives and government departments are through the Private Office of the Minister. I found that it was not unusual for elected representatives to go direct to civil servants. I issued an instruction that this was to cease. Some Northern Ireland civil servants disagreed with me when I was not prepared to allow Convention representatives to act as if they were Members of Parliament, or Members of an Assembly. I would have had problems with the Westminster MPs had I proceeded in this way.

The fact that the twenty-six local authorities have little power, that the area boards are non-elected, does mean that some civil servants are more in contact with the general public. They have a communication responsibility that is not so marked in Great Britain.

I found also that constituents in Northern Ireland tended to write to elected representatives other than those in their own constituencies. Catholic citizens would write to Catholic elected representatives, and Protestants to Protestant representatives. This tendency, to which there are exceptions, will last so long as the tribal base of political organizations lasts.

Through it all, the people of Northern Ireland had much more direct contact with Stormont than the people of Great Britain have with Whitehall. It was, and I have no doubt still is, common practice for individual citizens to telephone directly to the Secretary of State's office as they had to that of the Prime Minister in the past.

Indeed, Stormont Castle from early morning to late at night was a hive of activity. Delegations came at the shortest of notice. My room was open house in a way that it not possible in Whitehall.

During the first period of direct rule the Westminster Government set up an Advisory Council of nominated members. Those appointed were men and women of ability and motivated by the highest feelings of public service. It did not work. Nominated members may have been suitable in some forms of colonial government; it was not, and is not, suitable for Northern Ireland.

When the Government announced direct rule in 1972, on all sides of the House of Commons it was realized that there would be problems with Northern Irish legislation. Major bills, e.g., the Constitution Bill, of course passed through all the procedures of the House of Commons on the floor of the House. Less contentious but nevertheless important legislation was dealt with under the Northern Ireland Temporary Provisions Act, as it does now under successors. This means, bluntly, a one-and-a-half hour's debate as befits an order-in-Council, i.e., delegated legislation.

To allow a longer debate as often happens is one thing, but it does

53

not meet the need for proper parliamentary scrutiny. In my day as Secretary of State we set up a Northern Ireland Committee of the House of Commons so that the legislation could be discussed in draft before going to the floor of the House. This was an improvement.

The overall procedure was meant to be temporary until such time as Northern Ireland returned to devolved government. This has not proved possible and, at a time when the government is engaged in talks on the future, I say no more than that the parliamentary procedures are unsuitable for the long term.

Given the amount of legislation and its range into the field of local government, it is no answer to argue for treatment on a normal UK bill procedure. It is flying in the face of history and political reality to give extra power to the existing twenty-six local councils and thus remove direct responsibility from the Secretary of State and thus from Parliament.

What about Northern Ireland in the Cabinet? Except in times of crisis Northern Ireland does not loom large in its considerations and the main work is left to the Northern Ireland Committee of the Cabinet under whatever name successive governments give it. In practice, the responsibility falls almost completely to the Secretary of State allied closely with the Secretary of State for Defence.

In practice, the relationship with GOC on a day-to-day basis is the responsibility of the Secretary of State for Northern Ireland. Part of the job of the Secretary of State is to visit Lisburn frequently and to visit units in the field.

In my day, with the full support of the Foreign Secretary, the relationship with the South fell to the Secretary of State for Northern Ireland and discussions with the government of the South were normally a matter for the holder of that office. The government at Stormont before direct rule would have done better had bilateral discussions with the South taken place on a more consistent basis. In this respect successive governments in the Republic ignored the North for too long. I suppose discussions with the North would have smacked too much of acceptance of its existence. There was always, I should add, administrative contact between the Northern Ireland Ministries and their counterparts in Dublin.

Northern Ireland Ministers in my view have one of the most interesting jobs in Whitehall. Junior members have a role within the province and a range of responsibilities that they could not have in any other department. They become well known in Northern Ireland in their own right and are more than a political cog in the machine. The Secretary of State has an overall policy and administrative responsibility which cannot be repeated in most other departments.

The workload is enormous and the travelling involved, both within the province and between Northern Ireland and Great Britain, adds greatly to this. From time to time — as for example during the Ulster Workers Strike and periods of civil strife — the workload is much heavier.

As for myself, and for others I have no doubt, one can never get Northern Ireland out of one's system. My praise for all the civil servants there and particularly those in the NIO that I grew to know so well, is unstinted.

There is in Northern Ireland a hatred as shown by the bombings, the killings, the casualties. It is there and the scars will long remain. Nevertheless, and not for the sake of a peroration or for saying the right thing, there is far more to Northern Ireland than this. It is an exciting country, the people who live there are themselves, through its music and its art, a fine people.

Direct rule needs an understanding of this. We in London can play a part in government. Success will only come when the people of Northern Ireland govern themselves. The Stormont Constitution did not work and we will have to find something to replace it. The concept involved in 1922 however was the right one.

Direct rule can only be temporary. Its limitation is seen at times of constitutional crisis. I found in 1974 politicians who passionately wished to be part of the UK but equally passionately did not accept the logic of the political arithmetic involved in 12 seats (or 17) out of 635. The aim must be to return to devolved government in Belfast with the participation of both sides of the community.

This will not be easy, as the last decade has shown. There is no blueprint or plan to work from and all the time there is the Provisional IRA. We have come a long way from civil rights. Violence for the sake of it has become the order of the day. Under direct rule or devolved government this violence must be contained. It will only be defeated with the full co-operation of the Republic.

Discussion

Mr. Rees was asked to expand on his suggestion that Northern Ireland civil servants leaned to the majority, i.e. to the Protestant side. He said that with the new devolved administration this policy discrimination was not practised. He was not referring to individual cases. Inevitably, given the nature of place, with the old "Protestant" Parliament representing a Protestant people, the government was bound to have leaned in the direction of the majority community.

Asked why any politician should take on the "thankless" job of Secretary of State for Northern Ireland, Mr. Rees suggested that in practice it did not seem to have done its incumbents much subsequent harm. He had himself found that the interest and the challenge of the job made it difficult to relinquish. He had been offered the chance to change jobs on one occasion but had declined, particularly because he wished to see through the then impending changes in prosecution policy.

A questioner suggested that the schools bore a heavy responsibility in perpetuating the divisions between the communities in Northern Ireland, and asked how far Mr. Rees had felt that it might be possible to use the school system to bring about integration. He replied that the Protestant community had always favoured using the State schools. But it was a characteristically English idea to suppose that an approach which had worked perfectly well in post-war Germany would work in Northern Ireland. The two sides would come together only on their own terms. The only hope was to accept that there were two separate communities and to persuade them to respect each other. On the other hand, it was interesting to note how well the two communities appeared to integrate on neutral ground, for example, in Corby.

Manifestos and Mandarins

TONY BENN

The argument in outline

My thesis is a very simple one and can be briefly stated.

First, that the power, role, influence and authority of the senior levels of the civil service in Britain — especially now we are members of the EEC — have grown to such an extent as to create the embryo of a corporate state. This would threaten the workings of British democracy under which the people of this country are supposed to govern themselves through the Parliament they elect and the Ministers who are accountable to it.

Second, that the main responsibility for allowing this to happen must be shared by Parliament, by Ministers who have failed to speak out on this issue, and by successive Prime Ministers who have actually and positively encouraged this trend to bureaucracy because it reinforces the power of that office.

Third, that the time has come when major constitutional reforms are now urgently required. These must restore the authority of the House of Commons, secure effective ministerial control over the civil service and move towards a more constitutional type of premiership. We must also discuss the reforms necessary to bring all this about, openly, as a central part of our national political debate.

Ministerial relationships with officials

There are conflicts and tensions within our political system which receive a great deal of public attention. There are conflicts between the Government of the day, whichever it is, and the Opposition of the day. There are conflicts between the Government and Parliament, taken together by the electorate to mean "them" versus "us", the people. There are conflicts between the front benches of all parties and the back benches of all parties. There are conflicts between the elected Parliament and other centres of power in society. There are conflicts between Britain and other foreign governments or foreign interests. There are conflicts between parties. There are conflicts between class interests, as between capital and labour. There are conflicts of ideology, both internal and external. Each of these conflicts are quite familiar to political scientists and to the electorate as a whole.

But there is another relationship which has received far less public attention, except in ministerial memoirs and some specialized writing, that its importance justifies. That is, the actual working relationship and the balance of real power as it exists between Ministers, who have been elected to Parliament to implement the policy espoused by the majority, and the most senior permanent government officials within government departments who have the major responsibility for public administration.

The case for a public discussion

It is often argued that this relationship is one that should remain confidential and that it is not right to bring it out into the open. The reasons for maintaining secrecy are various. It is, for example, argued that it is in the national interest to preserve secrecy. Certainly there are areas of government which it is in the national interest to keep under the tightest veil of secrecy: for example, defence plans, security arrangements, budgetary decisions, position papers for international conferences, commercial arrangements, personal data and any other matter where the national interest is directly concerned. But the relationship in practice between different parts of the Constitution is a legitimate — indeed essential — subject for public discussion and understanding.

It is also argued that revelations about this relationship will undermine the confidence of those officials and Ministers who have to work together. It is true that in any relationship confidence must be maintained, and that that confidence requires a degree of personal trust, that those involved will exercise proper discretion in what they reveal at the time or later. But to extend that argument, which rests upon common sense and the decencies of personal relationships, to argue that the nature of that relationship itself should be concealed is to arange that the public has no right to know what goes on in its name and is completely insupportable.

Ministerial memoirs or diaries are often criticized on the grounds that they undermine that relationship of confidence. I cannot share that view. It may of course be embarrassing to be mentioned by name in such memoirs. But democracy must mean that a society can learn by experience; and if that experience and the lessons from it are to be concealed by secrecy, that learning process becomes much harder.

The danger of memoirs seem to me to lie in quite a different direction. It is that the high drama that occurs during some of the great Whitehall battles are often so exciting that the clashes between individuals may blank out the real issues — reinforcing the false idea that it is the personalities that matter and not the constitutional issues.

It is such gossip and malice that may undermine confidence, but not documented disclosure and proper analysis.

Civil servants sometimes argue that their special position makes it impossible for them to answer criticisms made of their conduct and it is therefore unfair to them to speak about their role. This argument, too, requires a proper response.

Properly presented, the case against civil service power does not hinge upon the conduct of civil servants as individuals, but upon the power granted to them by the Prime Minister or other Ministers. To that extent, there is no answer needed — except in so far as civil servants, exercising their rights as electors, may wish to argue that the balance of power between the civil service and Minister is right; or that any failure should be attributed to the weakness or errors of the Minister. And, as I hope to show, very senior civil servants have said just that in their own memoirs.

Indeed, the power of the civil service to arrange for its view of policy to be transmitted discreetly to the media is every bit as great as is the power of Ministers, and in the case of the Cabinet Office, the Treasury, the Foreign Office and the Home Office, this delicate briefing of top opinion-formers goes on on a regular basis.

It is true that the most dramatic leaks which hit the headlines usually come from Ministers in pursuit of their personal, political or departmental interests; and in particular, come from the Prime Minister of the day who, through Number 10, is responsible for 90% of all the leakes which occur. But having said that, the editor of *The Times*, the *Financial Times*, the *Daily Telegraph* and the heavy Sundays and weeklies and their most trusted and senior correspondents are rarely left in any doubt as to where the mandarins stand on any major policy issue.

The difference between ministerial leaks and official briefings is that Ministers often have an interest in letting their own role be known, whereas senior officials have an equal interest in preserving their anonymity.

The civil service and prime ministerial power

My knowledge of the civil service derives entirely from my own personal observations as a citizen, as a Member of Parliament and as a departmental Minister.

I have always been treated with great courtesy, both personally and in the handling of many thousands of constituency cases which have involved contact with the public service at various levels. There have been very few occasions indeed when either my constituents or I have had any grounds for complaint about the conduct of individual civil servants.

The public image of the faceless, humourless, unimaginative civil servant is a gross distortion of the truth. Like any big organization, public administration has its weaknesses and its failures. But in general, the civil service compares very well indeed in its conduct, its sense of responsibility, its dedication to the public welfare and its personal relations with the public, set alongside the behaviour of non-governmental organizations.

Moreover, the degree of accountability in the public services is far greater than exists in the private sector through the operation of market forces. All civil servants are Crown servants who see themselves in that capacity in their relationship with Ministers.

British governments are, in law, formed at the request of the Sovereign by an individual who is invited to form an administration, subject to his or her capacity to secure a parliamentary majority to support it. Thus, the Prime Minister of the day is the head of that administration and his or her personal authority is the only authority explicitly ceded by the Crown to an individual.

The civil service accepts that authority and works under it and through it. All Prime Ministers then consolidate their authority over the civil service by taking over two key ministerial positions — that of the First Lord of the Treasury, which controls finance, and that of Minister for the Civil Service, which controls appointments. It is, thus, in the interests of the civil service to serve the Prime Minister of the day; and in the interests of the Prime Minister to have a strong civil service to support his or her personal authority.

All the issues of importance concerning the role, power, influence and authority of the civil service thus take you right back to the alliance of mutual loyalty and support between Number 10 Downing Street and the mandarins. And nothing whatever can be done to change the present structure of power unless it changes the nature of that alliance by altering the power of the Prime Minister.

Other Ministers are, of course, appointed by the Prime Minister and require the formal approval of the Crown, but they hold their offices at the pleasure of the Prime Minister. So do the Permanent Secretaries, who enjoy a greater security of tenure and can and do regard the Secretaries of State and departmental Ministers they serve as birds of passage, who like them, are expected to work for the Prime Minister. If the Prime Minister retains real personal confidence in the Ministers whom he or she appoints, then the Permanent Secretaries know it is in their interests to support them. But if the permanent officials have reason to believe that the Prime Minister has lost confidence in their departmental Minister, it is in their interest to by-pass him and his policies.

Moreover, the Permanent Secretary's network within Whitehall, in which the Secretary of the Cabinet is a key figure, can work very effectively to undermine the confidence of the Prime Minister in a Minister, whom the civil service dislike or distrust; and thus create an atmosphere favourable to a by-pass situation in which the Minister concerned can be slowed down, deflected, diverted, obstructed, or in the end, reshuffled or removed. It is very important that this should be clearly understood, because it places the main responsibility for making the necessary changes where that responsibility belongs — in the hands of the Prime Minister — and it makes intelligible the conduct of senior civil servants in their relationship with their Minister.

It also indicates that any reform of the work of the civil service would require a major change in the powers of the Prime Minister, as I believe it does. Such a reform is unlikely to be welcome to any incumbent of that office, or to the senior civil service. But it could be secured by public pressure through Parliament or the political parties.

The mandarins in modern Britain work as closely with the Emperor or Empress who governs from Downing Street as can ever have occurred in ancient China. Together they control the real levers of state power, many of which are so secret that most Cabinet Ministers do not even know of their existence, let alone how they are being operated.

The role of the manifesto in a democracy

For the administrative class of the civil service the problems of government are necessarily seen from the top and from the inside where power resides. But for the electorate as a whole, the system is seen from below and from the outside. There are pressing needs to be met, injustices to be corrected and problems to be solved, and the ballot box is the main instrument for securing political change.

Seen from that viewpoint, the agglomeration of state power at the top and the secrecy with which it is surrounded is often seen as a major barrier to industrial, economic, social and political advance.

The Labour movement was established to shift the balance of power in favour of working people and their families. Labour history can only be understood in those terms. First, the struggle for free trade unions reflected in the campaigns against the Combination Acts. Then, the Chartist campaigns to extend the vote to working people, followed by the Suffragette movement to win the vote for women. In parallel with this came the establishment first of the Labour Representation Committee and then the Labour Party, and in 1918 the adoption of Socialist objectives.

In each election since then the specific programme for the following Parliament has been embodied in a manifesto put before the electorate for endorsement, with a view to implementation if a mandate is given. Thus, the manifesto, into which an enormous amount of detailed work has gone, once it has been adopted by the party leadership and endorsed by the electorate, becomes the key link between the people and political power.

It is the belief that real change can be made peacefully through the machinery of Parliament and the work of Labour Ministers that makes the British Labour Party democratic and explains why it has never adopted violent revolution as its instrument for social change.

It is, thus, of central importance for the maintenance of confidence in our system of government that that process of social change can be made to work effectively and that the manifesto is taken seriously by Members of Parliament, Ministers and senior officials responsible for implementing it.

It is to that process of implementation that I now want to turn. For it is at the very moment when a successful party, with a manifesto, sends its Ministers into office that the role of the senior civil service comes into play.

Whitehall and consensus politics

How do the Permanent Secretaries view this process of party policy-making? It would be a mistake to suppose — as some socialists have suggested — that the senior ranks of the civil service are active Conservatives posing as impartial administrators.

The issue is not their personal political views, nor their preferences for particular governments, though as citizens they are perfectly entitled to hold such views and to vote accordingly. The problem arises from the fact that the civil service sees itself as being above the party battle, with a political position of its own to defend against all-comers, including incoming governments armed with their philosophy and programme.

Civil service policy — and there is no other way to describe it — is an amalgam of views that have been developed over a long period of time and in the development of which the civil service itself has played a notable role. It draws some of its force from a deep commitment to the benefits of continuity and a fear that adversary politics may lead to sharp reversals by incoming governments of policies devised by their predecessors, which the civil service played a great part in developing. To that extent, the Permanent Secretaries could be held to prefer consensus politics and hope they would remain the basis for all policy and administration.

As the word implies, consensus politics draw their inspiration from many sources in all political parties. The post-war consensus, which ended during the 1970s, was based upon the foundation laid by the Liberal Government of 1906 and especially the work of Lloyd George at the Treasury and Churchill and Beveridge at the Board of Trade, who began the welfare state. It was added to by patient Fabian social planners and enriched by the bold interventionism advocated by Harold Macmillan in his book *The Middle Way* published in 1938.

Consensus politics was institutionalized during the war-time coalition, in which Winston Churchill, Clement Attlee and Sir Archibald Sinclair worked together with Ministers like Sir John Anderson who had been a Permanent Secretary himself. Despite the heated political debates of the 1950s and 1960s this broad consensus remained, in that the disagreements between the parties were contained within the framework of agreed objectives, i.e. full employment and welfarism; and the differences were largely then confined to the question of which party was to be privileged to administer this corpus of policy. This was the heyday of Butskellism.

The civil service laboured long and hard in support of this approach and helped to construct a top level corporate structure of committees and quangos, which brought together all those who could be persuaded to share their desire for the minimum of public controversy that is compatible with the acceptance of the two-and-a-half party system. Thus, when the senior civil servants see a new government come into power with a policy that goes outside that consensus, there is an anxiety at the possible effect upon their policy; and plans are laid that would have the effect of containing this new surge of political power and diverting ministerial energies into safer channels that do not disturb the even flow of established Whitehall policy.

The real political views of senior permanent officials are not normally made public. Any Minister quickly becomes aware of them by careful reading of the papers submitted to him by his own civil servants and in the flood of telegrams from our ambassadors abroad, which are widely circulated to Ministers.

Some retired civil servants are willing to express their own views on the governments which they have served, as Lord Armstrong has done. But it is rare for a leak of an actual government paper to take place. That is why, when it does, it merits very careful study.

Last spring Sir Nicholas Henderson's farewell despatch from the Paris Embassy was leaked to the *Economist* and it provides a classic and typical insight into the mind of the Foreign Office and Whitehall, corresponding closely to those expressed by the advocates of the proposed new centre party in Britain; hostile to the trade unions, passionately committed to the EEC, and pessimistic about the future of Britain.

Day after day, week after week, and month after month, the same analysis is fed to Ministers and it would be surprising if it did not have an influence. Its influence is all the greater because all these papers and despatches are heavily classified and the public do not know what officials really think, cannot challenge their analysis and are continually assured that the mandarins are politically neutral, which they are not.

Civil service influence in practice

I have seen this process of civil service containment successfully practiced against both Conservative and Labour governments over the last thirty years.

The bold challenge of the 1964 Labour Government, with its "new Britain" manifesto, was absorbed and defused by July 20, 1966, when the Treasury persuaded the then Chancellor to insist upon a package of economic measures that killed the national plan and instituted a statutory pay policy. It happened again when the 1970 Conservative Government was driven off its commitment to the philosophy developed at Selsdon Park and the then Prime Minister was persuaded to do a U-turn which took him back to the same policies that Macmillan had developed from 1962 to 1963, and that Wilson had been persuaded to follow from 1966 to 1970.

It happened again after the referendum in 1975, when the Labour Government was persuaded to abandon its 1974 manifesto and was diverted back to the policies of 1972-1974, as pursued by Heath. It will be interesting to see how long it is before the same pressures are successful in guiding Mrs. Thatcher back to the well-trodden paths followed on the advice of the civil service by Macmillan, Wilson, Heath, and Wilson.

It would, of course, be quite wrong to attribute all these policy changes to civil service pressures alone. All Ministers must take responsibility for what they do and all are subject to a wide range of other pressures besides those which come from Whitehall. But it is not a coincidence that governments of both parties appear to end up with policies very similar to each other, and which are in every case a great deal more acceptable to Whitehall than were the manifestos upon which they were originally elected.

It is also true that the central theme of consensus, or Whitehall, policies which have been pursued by governments of all parties for the last twenty years or more have been accompanied by a steady decline in Britain's fortunes, which has now accelerated into a near catastrophic collapse of our industrial base. The governments which followed these policies — especially 1964, 1970, 1974 and 1979 — have paid a heavy price in electoral terms, whilst those who furnished the briefing for the Ministers concerned have continued in power, subject only to the normal wastage occasioned by retirement at 60.

Whatever the future may hold for this Government, a new centre party is being promised which it appears will be dedicated to the pursuit of those same failed policies.

Apart from some ministerial memoirs, and a few interesting revelations by retired civil servants, there has been no real examination of the role of the civil service during this period, or the methods it uses to secure ministerial compliance with its policies. It is to these methods that I now wish to turn.

The civil service at its best

Where Whitehall agrees with what Ministers wish to do it can give formidable and effective assistance in the execution of policy. I can think of many occasions during my own ministerial life when such help was unstintingly given and with results that could not possibly have been achieved without it.

Whitehall, when it bends its mind to secure an agreed objective, is first-class in every respect. One such example I recite from my experience to prove that point — in the execution of the last Government's oil policy, as set out in its 1974 manifesto. As Secretary of State for Energy I could and did rely completely upon the dedicated work of those senior officials who had responsibility for securing the compliance of the international oil companies with our requirements for 51 per cent participation, for the build up of BNOC, and for the increase of the Petroleum Revenue Tax.

I must also add that the role of a Minister's Private Office is of crucial importance, and I have enjoyed full support from a succession of Principal Private Secretaries, who occupy a most delicate position between the ministerial and official hierarchies within the Department, poised between personal loyalty to the Minister whilst discharging their duties as officials. Without a helpful Private Office, no Minister would survive for five minutes in the battles that surge through Whitehall. I must pay tribute to the help given and believe that an expanded Private Office could form the basis of a real ministerial Cabinet.

How the civil service gets its way

The senior ranks of the civil service include people of the highest intelligence, with a great deal of experience of government, and with direct access to all the centres of power and influence in this country, in Europe, in the USA, and in many other places. They are strongly organized within Whitehall through a network of official committees, co-ordinated by the Cabinet Office under the general direction of the Secretary of the Cabinet, the most powerful figure of them all. The minutes of these committees are not circulated to Ministers who are in general wholly ignorant about what is discussed, when, by whom, and with what effect. The civil service as a whole accept this process as very natural; and since their own promotion depends upon the approval of their most senior colleagues, they tend to follow the lead given from above.

It is necessary at some stage in this lecture to list explicitly the techniques that are used by Whitehall to get its own way. These techniques have emerged in some ministerial memoirs, or other books and articles by those who have had first-hand experience of what goes on at the highest levels of Cabinet policy-making. Unfortunately, the revelations are usually so dramatic that they obscure the techniques themselves. Let me therefore list those methods broadly.

Determined mandarins have the power, and sometimes use it, to adopt some of all of the following methods:

a. by briefing Ministers

The document prepared by officials for presentation to incoming Ministers after a general election comes in two versions, one for each major party. A similar document is produced after a reshuffle. It is a very important document that has attracted no public interest, and it is presented to a Minister at the busiest moment of his life — when he enters his department and is at once bombarded by decisions to be made, the significance of which he cannot at that moment appreciate.

The brief may thus be rapidly scanned and put aside for a proper reading when the pressure eases, which it rarely does. In fact this brief repays the most careful scrutiny because from it can be deduced the real policy of the department which officials hope the new Minister will follow. It may be dressed up to look like a range of options for implementing his manifesto, but beneath that presentational language it reveals the departmental view.

For example the 172-page Department of Energy brief for in-coming Labour Ministers in 1974, several of the 35 sections of which were marked "secret" or "confidential", included one sentence I want to quote: "In principal it is desirable that all new orders for base load power stations should be nuclear." In fact this policy was not followed by the Labour Government which ordered the DRAX B coal-fired station, but the brief correctly forecast both the sustained civil service opposition to the ordering of DRAX B, and also forecast the recent policy announcement of the present Government on nuclear power made late last year.

That is only one example, and there are many others. In October 1974 after the second general election I was reappointed to the Department of Industry, and one of the briefing sheets in the package was headed "For an in-coming Labour Minister — if not Mr. Benn" — which indicated a premature hope of the reshuffle that occurred nine months later. It however gave me a useful insight into the policy which the Department hoped my successor would follow — as indeed he did.

I believe that academic research on the full set of briefs prepared by the civil service for Ministers in all departments in all governments when they enter office and throughout their term since the war would offer a more accurate explanation of policies followed and why, than a similar study of the manifestos upon which each government was elected.

b. by setting the framework of policy

The key to civil service influence lies in its power to set the framework of policy. Lord Armstrong wrote very frankly about this power as quoted in *The Times:*

> "Obviously I had a great deal of influence. The biggest and most pervasive influence is in setting the framework within which questions of policy are raised. We, while I was at The Treasury, had a framework of the economy basically neo-Keynesian. We set the questions which we asked Ministers to decide arising out of that framework and it would have been enormously difficult for any Minister to change the framework, so to that extent we had great power."

Thus Ministers are continually guided to reach their decisions within that framework. Those Ministers who seek to open up options beyond that framework are usually unable to get their proposals seriously considered.

c. by the control of information

The flow of necessary information to a Minister on a certain subject can be made selective, in other ways restricted, delayed until it is too late or stopped altogether.

Sir William Hayter, a distinguished former ambassador, wrote this in a letter to *The Times* of January 14 this year:

> "The temptation to conceal from an unreasonable Minister facts

which might tempt to confirm him in his unreason must have been very strong."

Geoffrey Moorhouse in *The Diplomats,* his recent book on the Foreign Office, was even more explicit in describing the renegotiations that preceded the EEC referendum:

"Some of the home civil servants in the delegation from time to time quite deliberately kept their own Departments in London ignorant of what was going on in Brussels for a delicately balanced day or two, or even for a few vital hours. This was not a betrayal of Whitehall; it simply meant that what Whitehall did not know Whitehall could not pass on."

I can confirm all that from my own experience in relation to a number of critical issues involving foreign policy, economic and industrial policy and civil nuclear policy. The breaking of the oil sanctions on Rhodesia, the use of movements against sterling, the protection of Treasury control of BP, the campaign for pressurized water reactors and many other issues were dealt with in this way.

One example comes to mind over defence. The first draft of the Defence White Paper that came to one Cabinet I attended showed such a large gap in the military balance between East and West as to arouse questioning. It turned out that in calculating the military strength of the West the Ministry of Defence had left out the French armed forces. When questioned the reason given was that NATO did not exercise the same operational control over the French forces as applied to the rest of the alliance. In fact, of course, this crude misinformation was designed to win public support for a bigger defence budget by suggesting a more serious imbalance than existed. The Ministry of Defence were instructed to put the French back into the White Paper charts and they did. But it was fortunate that someone had spotted it in time. The attempt to mislead Cabinet, Parliament and public was inexcusable.

d. by the mobilization of Whitehall

It is also easy for the civil service to stop a Minister by mobilizing a whole range of internal forces against his policy.

The attempt by the then Foreign Secretary in 1975 to secure a separate seat for Britain at the North-South dialogue on energy was systematically undermined by the Foreign Office which made no secret of its hostility to any move which might weaken its support for a common EEC stance.

The normal method of mobilizing Whitehall opposition is for officials to telephone their colleagues in other departments to report what a Minister is proposing to do, thus stimulating a flow of letters from other Ministers (drafted for them by their officials) asking to be consulted, calling for inter-departmental committees to be set up, all in the hope that an unwelcome initiative can be nipped in the bud or transferred to the safety of an official examination.

The techniques used include the preparation of statistics upon undisclosed assumptions such as an exaggeration of costs — used to delay the implementation of the health and safety legislation. There may be a warning that "lawyers advise that it would require legislation" following by a second warning that "the legislative timetable is so crowded that the measure is unlikely to get into the Queen's Speech in the foreseeable future".

Ministers can be briefed against each other. I will give some examples.

I recall one very minor occasion when Lord Brown (formerly Wilfred Brown of Glacier Metal) was Minister of State at the Board of Trade and wrote to me as Minister of Technology. My Private Secretary came to warn me that Lord Brown's letter had been written by him personally and did not reflect the views of the Department. This warning was presumably to alert me to disregard it. Actually it served to remind me that the civil service did not expect Ministers to go beyond the advice of their officials and had ways of preventing any such initiatives from being successful.

In October 1977 a very senior official at the Department of Industry minuted his Secretary of State to alert him to an initiative I was taking about the restructuring of the turbine generator industry. This minute was shown to me and it recommended a way of blocking my initiative and a draft that would do it. The minute then went on: "If, however, you feel that you need to take a more active line in order to avoid being upstaged by Mr. Benn, then the letter at E5 would be appropriate."

One of the most amusing examples occurred when my own Permanent Secretary in one department was violently opposed to a course of action I had decided to adopt. He knew that the matter would come up at a Cabinet Committee attended both by me and by a junior Minister of my own department whom he rightly thought was more sympathetic to his view. He therefore briefed this junior Minister against my view. Unfortunately the junior Minister concerned actually read out what he had been given and said that he ought to tell his colleagues that the Permanent Secretary did not agree with what the Secretary of State was advocating. Everyone looked rather embarrassed at this tactless revelation of what was going on.

e. by the mobilization of external pressure

If Ministers require more pressure than can be generated internally then other resources may have to be brought into play.

A telegram from an embassy abroad can be elicited to give a warning of the consequences that would flow from the pursuit of a certain course of action. NATO, the EEC or even the views of multinational companies or international bankers may be cited in support of a line of policy.

The IMF may actually have been informally encouraged to put pressure for public expenditure cuts upon the last Labour Cabinet, and I believe it was.

And these techniques can easily be reinforced by domestic pressures through the press. I am certainly not suggesting anything as crude as a direct appeal to the Editor of *The Times,* the *Telegraph* or the *Economist.* But such an appeal would not be necessary since the mandarins and the media proprietors share the same analysis and the same social values and the same interests which at certain critical junctures can be very useful.

f. by the use of expertise

Most of my life has been in the departments which have a high technical content — Post Office, Technology, Power, Industry and Energy. It is the task of Ministers in such departments to interrogate their officials and the experts responsible until the political issues can be disentangled from the technical one.

Any lay Minister will start at a disadvantage in dealing with such matters. It would be a mistake to suppose that senior officials are any more expert than an experienced Minister. They may, however, seek to persuade a Minister that the experts must be right and that such technical decisions are non-political.

I recall receiving a long minute in my Friday box in July 1966 advocating the expenditure of many tens of millions of pounds on two new scientific projects — the High Flux Beam Reactor (HFBR) and the High Magnetic Field Laboratory (HMFL). My Permanent Secretary had written "I agree" and put his initials below. I laboured over the paper all weekend, and in the end decided to ask him to give me the reasons why this huge sum of money should be spent on these projects. Not having received a satisfactory answer I vetoed them. It was just a bounce and it had failed.

Nine years later a similar incident occurred. A paper was put before me to put before the Cabinet Committee recommending one or two courses of action on the fast breeder reactor. Option I was to build the fast breeder at a cost of about £2 billion. Option 2 was to pay about £1.5 billion for a watching brief which would allow us to be ready to build one later. Colleagues turned both options down, and the Cabinet Office which had master-minded the operation realized that it had over-egged the pudding.

Sir William Hayer in his recent letter to *The Times* argued that:

"There can be no question of a manifesto commitment as between alternative nuclear reactors. And if expert opinion in this field is unanimous in favour of a particular course, is it likely that a Minister, and one without any scientific qualifications, would be right and all the experts wrong?"

This argument amounts to a declaration that democratic control cannot extend to technical matters and is only tolerable in the shrinking areas of policy that laymen can comprehend. It is a recipe for technocracy and the transfer of power to non-elected laymen in the persons of the mandarins.

g. by the use of the CPRS

One important innovation in Whitehall was the establishment of the CPRS which was intended to provide the focus for a broader, longer and more detached view of policy than could be obtained from departmental Ministers or officials heavily pressed by the burden of on-going business.

Though this idea of a think tank has certain superficial attractions, it has in the event turned out to be a very different body. Those recruited into it include both civil servants and outsiders, and it has in practice become a powerful lobby for the Cabinet Secretary himself to whom it is responsible. The quality of its work reflects its small staffing. It is much more avowedly political in its opinions and the head of it sits in Cabinet Committees with the status of a Cabinet Minister able to circulate papers and to speak.

The CPRS should be put under a Minister or disbanded altogether. Ministers should make time to be their own think tank and each government should see its own party colleagues outside government as the best agency for stimulating its thoughts about the future.

h. by the use of patronage

One extra source of power available to the civil service lies in its strategic command of patronage.

Most public attention is focused upon the mere handful of appointments that are specifically in ministerial control. The use, or abuse, of the Honours List, or the charge of "jobs for the boys" when a party colleague is given a major post, attracts a great deal of press attention. But thousands of run-of-the-mill appointments to nationalized industries and quangos of one kind or another come from civil service lists and reflect civil service preferences, even if only because Ministers are too busy to concern themselves with such appointments.

Thus the civil service exercises an influence far beyond the confines of Whitehall, and can call upon the resources of its own appointees when it is necessary to do so.

i. by the use of national security

Another power available to the civil service is the use of security arrangements. MI5 reports to the Home Secretary and MI6 to the Foreign Secretary, and the Prime Minister exercises supreme responsibilities.

How close the control of these services by the Ministers responsible really is only those who hold those offices will know. But published information suggests that it may not be very effective. The Maxwell-Fyffe directive of 1952 suggests that the Home Secretary is only brought in when MI5 wish to seek his advice.

> "You and your staff will maintain well-established convention whereby Ministers do not concern themselves with detailed information which may be obtained by the Security Service in particular cases, but are furnished with such information only as may be necessary for the determination of any issue on which guidance is sought."

Sir George Young, former head of MI6, recently said on BBC Radio 4: "The higher reaches of the civil service undoubtedly make most of the decisions for Ministers and put them in front of them and say 'Minister do you agree?" It is, therefore, interesting to read that Barbara Castle records in her diary for October 31, 1968 that: "Another glorious document has been circulated to me by our Security boys on the attitudes of the Communist Party during the engineering negotiations."

It is widely believed that the trade union movement is subjected to very widespread surveillance. My own limited experience on the fringe of these matters suggests that surveillance in Britain goes far beyond any justifiable definition of subversion and constitutes a secret control over political thought and action which is well within the legitimate range of democratic activity, and as such constitutes a very powerful source of civil service power.

The Common Market — buttress for bureaucracy

Britain's membership of the Common Market has had the most

profound influence upon our whole Constitution and method of government.

Much public attention has been paid to the philosophy embodied in the Treaty of Rome, to the unfair budgetary contribution and to the absurdities of the Common Agricultural Policy. But the impact upon our own system of government has passed with very little comment. Yet British entry marked the most profound change in our system of government since 1066, or perhaps since the withdrawl of the Romans in 410.

We now have a written Constitution, a Constitutional Court and are governed by Ministers who legislate in secret, but can only enact legislation prepared by a commission, made up of politicians appointed to be civil servants who enjoy the powers of both breeds. Whitehall is now busy adapting itself to these new arrangements and doing so with real zest. The Common Market is a mandarin's paradise. Not only has real power over many sectors of policy been transferred from London (where Ministers work) to Brussels or Luxembourg (which Ministers only visit), but the head of COREPER is a permanent official working direct to the Foreign Office. Parliament is no longer sovereign and can thus be pushed into the background as far as the laws are concerned. If by chance British legislation were to conflict with EEC legislation, the latter would be upheld by the European Court and enforced by the British courts whatever Parliament said.

Every item of EEC legislation is executed under the royal prerogative of treaty-making powers and is first negotiated by officials, often leaving Ministers with a mere power to approve or disapprove the package as a whole. As a result, the infection of Common Market bureaucracy has spread back into the heart of Whitehall from the source of the virus itself in Brussels.

The permanent secretaries who masterminded the preparatory work for all these activities through the Cabinet Office and the Foreign Office have now got a legitimate excuse to bypass and override departmental Ministers in the interests of co-ordination and the need to be good Europeans. Unless this process is stopped in its tracks, Britain could be governed by a commission of Permanent Secretaries and Ministers reduced to ciphers able only to accept or reject what is put before them. The House of Commons will be a consultative assembly which can express its opinions but do little more.

To go into this in any detail would take too long, but it cannot be long before the British people realize that in the space of a generation this country has been transformed from being the centre of our own world-wide empire to being a colony in someone else's European empire; heavily taxed, externally controlled and governed by a form of indirect rule, on behalf of an imperial commission on the continent.

In saying that, I must acknowledge that a clear majority of the

British Parliament voted for entry; and so did a clear majority of the electors in a national referendum. In the face of such an authoritative expression of British opinion, the civil service could legitimately argue that they were loyally implementing the decision reached. But it is not as simple as that. Geoffrey Moorhouse in his book is more explicit in identifying the role of the Foreign Office before the referendum. The following three quotations from his book, *The Diplomats*, are of the greatest public importance:

> "There was absolute commitment to the work in hand, complete devotion to standing fast in the market. The renegotiation of terms, quite obviously, would have failed without them. The result of the referendum might easily have gone the other way, too. There is a percentage of any national vote which expresses a gut reaction of many people who are beyond the immediate influence of evidence and argument; the crucial voters are those who can be swayed this way or that by the tides of political presentation right up to the moment of ballot. It would be difficult to overestimate the influence on that floating vote of the civil service alliance in Whitehall, combined with the activity of the British Delegation in Brussels."

Later in the same chapter Moorhouse describes the way the civil service worked at that time:

> "They saw it as legitimate and perfectly honourable practice to throw all their weight behind the emphasis on remaining in the Market, and to frustrate any attempts to turn the emphasis in the opposite direction. The codes of civil service say that at all times you support your own Minister in any conflict with another branch of the government. That rule went overboard in Brussels."

Finally, in the most revealing passage of all, Moorhouse says this:

> "The diplomats have a concept of grand alliance which includes the integration of all things national. The economic fusion will be followed by the financial, then the political. They do not doubt this for a moment: they see it as their job to help the process along."

I believe that this assessment is correct. Many people consider that some of the most senior civil servants — and especially those in the Foreign Office — are in the process of transferring their real allegiance from the United Kingdom to the European Communities. If that is so, the sooner the British people realize it the sooner they will understand what is happening to Britain and why.

The role of secrecy

Over all that I have described an official curtain of secrecy is supposed to be maintained. Why?

Everyone who has worked in Whitehall as a Minister or senior official knows very well what goes on and indeed may regard it as highly effective and praiseworthy. But the public at large are not officially permitted to know until 30 years later. True, the curtain of secrecy is regularly punctured by "leaks" and they cannot usually be authenticated or traced. Memoirs are documented but they come too late to alter the course of events.

Despite all this, secrecy is effective in preserving the anonymity of most mandarins and the security of the papers they write. The public is effectively excluded from knowing what is going on when they might have some influence on events by studying and challenging officials briefs and putting alternatives forward.

In whose interests is it that this secrecy should remain? It is in the interests both of weak Ministers and strong civil servants, both of whom prefer to keep the public in the dark. Weak Ministers because they dare not invite challenges to their policy which they fear they could not answer; strong civil servants because their strength lies in that they cannot be challenged if they can remain anonymous.

Why Ministers accept civil service power

It is sometimes said that a strong Minister can always get his way with his department and that all criticisms made by Ministers about the civil service are a confession of weakness and an excuse for failure. But the problem is much deeper than that.

In the examples I have given I am not seeking to allocate blame nor make any excuses for failure. I want to explain how the system actually works as I experienced it. Why do Ministers accept all this? It is a good question.

Lord Armstrong in the passage that I have quoted on his work at the Treasury wrote this:

> "We were very ready to explain it to anybody who was interested, but most Ministers were not interested, were just prepared to take the questions as we offered them, which came out of that framework without going back into the preconceptions of them."

I suppose that is another way of saying that many Ministers are happy to take the line of least resistance. Some Ministers are genuinely persuaded that what they are advised to do by their civil servants involves facing "the harsh realities" and telling the people "the truth however unpalatable it may be".

75

But whether the responsibility for allowing civil service power to be as great as it is lies with the Prime Minister, as I believe it does, with Ministers who are partly responsible, or with a civil service who uses that power with such skill and effectiveness, the fact remains that the power is great and that its exercise raises questions of major public interest.

The corporate state — a new form of feudalism

Ministers who have held office, as I have done, have a responsibility to describe it as it is, to point to its weaknesses and dangers and to recommend political reforms that would reduce or remove those dangers.

I have reached the solemn conclusion that what we have constructed in Britain is the embryo of a corporate state that more resembles feudalism than the democracy of which we often boast. Indeed the hierarchical character of the old feudalism which made its landlords into peers has been buttressed by adding bankers, industrialists, trade union leaders, ex-Ministers and ex-Permanent Secretaries to the Upper Chamber with an effective delaying veto over legislation from the elected Commons where that is thought necessary to defend their interest.

British corporatism, controlling a state function many times greater in real terms than it was fifty years ago, is, of course, quite different from that developed in central Europe between the wars which went fascist; and it is not at all the same as the corporate state set up by Stalin to build communism. British corporatism has come into being to sustain a fast-declining mixed economy and to seek to revitalize capitalism within the framework of a European union committed to that same end, hoping for the prosperity and super power status. In this scenario of a British colony within a European super-state civil servants will be in charge, at the centre of a complex network of power structures representing industry, finance, the army, security services and possibly even the leaders of European labour unions, if they can be inveigled in to join the club as associate members.

I am certain that there are millions of people — and I am one of them — who would not accept such a development. But if it is to be prevented, we must set ourselves new objectives and discuss them. In conclusion, it is to those objectives that I now want to turn.

A strategy for reform

If we are to reopen the campaign for democracy, certain things must be considered urgently.

a. A Freedom of Information Act — providing for a statutory right of access to knowledge about government and its workings, subject only to the accepted safeguards for information which it is in the national interest to keep secret.

b. Stronger parliamentary control — by the development of select committees to probe into the heart of Whitehall policy-making, including finance, foreign policy, defence and the security services.

c. A constitutional premiership — by making the Prime Minister much more accountable than he or she now is for the powers exercised and by moving towards a more genuine form of collective ministerial responsibility.

d. More ministerial control over the civil service — to secure compliance with the policies that Ministers were elected to implement. Proposals to this end have been widely discussed and would certainly involve making the most senior officials in each department more responsible to the Ministers whom they serve.

e. The abolition of patronage — by substituting advertisement, open selection, election or parliamentary confirmation procedures to cover all public appointments.

f. The amendment of Section 2 of the European Communities Act — to restore full law-making and tax-gathering powers to the elected House of Commons and the substitution of a new basis of European co-operation by accepting that this must rest upon a willingness of fully self-governing states to work together.

Conclusion — the case for democracy

In considering these issues, we do not want to find new scapegoats or pile the blame upon Ministers or civil servants who have let the system grow into what it is. What matters now is that we should examine what has happened to our system of government with fresh eyes and resolve to re-introduce constitutional democracy to Britain, so that the policies in the future will reflect the aspirations of our own people and not just the interests of some mandarins, some Ministers or some Members of Parliament who now seem to be strangely satisfied with the status quo.

In a period of rapid technical change it is essential that the machinery of government at all levels should be capable of reflecting the desires of the people expressed through the ballot box more expeditiously than is now the case. Indeed, it must, if we are to maintain the stability of our society.

The Decision Makers

SHIRLEY WILLIAMS

Where does power in Britain actually reside? Does it reside with Ministers, in turn responsible to an elected Parliament, as constitutional doctrine decrees? Does it reside with the civil service, which sees Ministers come and go, but itself goes on for ever? Or is it to be found somewhere different from either of these?

It is a very difficult question; I have thought about it for a long time, including during my fifteen years in Parliament, and the ten concurrent ones in government, and I still find the answer elusive. British civil servants obviously feel at least a qualified loyalty to their elected masters. But there have been some notable examples where that loyalty was disregarded. The famous Crichel Down case of 1954 involved civil servants at the Ministry of Agriculture improperly retaining land at Crichel Down which had been originally requisitioned for military purposes and should have been returned to its rightful owner. The Minister, Sir Thomas Dugdale, had not been informed and knew nothing about the matter. However, being a gentleman of the old school who accepted the doctrine of ministerial responsibility, he resigned.

Much more recently, in 1979, discussion of the case of Sir Anthony (now Mr.) Blunt, a self-confessed spy for the Soviet Union, revealed that his 1964 confession and the decision to allow him to keep both his title and his job as an artistic adviser to the Queen was neither reported to, nor agreed by, the Prime Minister of the day or his senior colleagues. Such an extraordinary and indeed unconstitutional occurrence is possible only if senior civil servants see themselves as running the country and making the decisions — the view that Ministers are merely public relations men and women whose job is to present the government's policies to Parliament, press and people.

I do not myself believe that many senior civil servants subscribe to this view, although I have met a few eminent ones who do. Civil servants like a strong lead from the top, even if they then react against it. Government, like nature, abhors a vacuum. Given a lack of leadership, civil servants fill the gap; given what they regard as wrong-headed leadership, they will argue and even obstruct, but will finally conform.

There are certain features of the British civil service that may help to create the inner confidence, even the hubris, on which the view-point I have described could be founded. The British civil service, despite some rather half-hearted recent reforms, continues to be recruited from a narrow base. Of administrative trainees (entering the highest grade) about one-fifth come from serving officers in the executive grade; the rest are recruited from outside, are almost always graduates, and 75% of them came in 1975 from two universities alone, Oxford and Cambridge. This in turn biases the service towards young men and women who attended public schools, since the public schools are still responsible for more than half Cambridge's undergraduates, and nearly half of Oxford's. Admittedly, many Oxbridge graduates apply for civil service positions, but surely the Civil Service Commission could make greater efforts to attract applicants from a wider range of higher education institutions?

Not only is the civil service recruited from a narrow base. It still takes on few people from outside either as late recruits or as secondments for a limited period, despite the urgings of the Fulton Committee. There are few exchanges between the civil service and industry, between the civil service and the professions, or even between the civil service and the even larger local government service. The civil service remains inbred. This allows it to establish and maintain its own internal norms, and its own internal hierarchy. It keeps promotion, demotion and discipline very much within its own hands. And it has to its credit high standards of probity, of behaviour and of service, despite a few large and disturbing lapses. It also has some excellent management practices: searching and demanding interviewing techniques, regular reporting on each individual's progress and achievement, the reports being discussed with their subject; considerable responsibility for men and women in their early twenties, if they show promise. But this controlled and relatively inbred structure has great weaknesses as well.

Experiencing little of the world outside government, the civil service does not understand industry. More disturbing, it does not even seem to want to. Hence its interventions in industry are often heavy-handed and inappropriate. (The same criticism, of course, can be made of some MPs and Ministers.) Unlike the French civil service, many of whose brilliant (and even *more* inbred) Enarques whiz through to the top in administration and then go on in their fifties to run French industry, civil servants rarely move into or from British industry. When they retire, their destination is more likely to be the City, banking and insurance. Businessmen rarely enter the administration, except fitfully as members of commissions or committees advising on a particular issue. When they do, they are rarely successful, but this reflects more on the gap between the attitudes and experience of administration and of industry than on themselves — and indeed, on the frightening and rigid compartmentalization of our society.

There has been some slight movement otwards giving young civil servants some experience of "the world out there", the world of the public they serve. In the Department of Employment, administrative trainees work for a short period in employment offices or Jobcentres; DHSS officials may spend a few months in social security offices. But it is the nature of such departments that they are close to the public. Treasury and Home Office men are rarely seen interviewing taxpayers or helping out at the immigration counters at the airports.

Hierarchical, large, well disciplined, inbred management structures are excellent for the carrying out of orders, and for the execution of policy, according to exponents of management techniques. They are much less effective as innovators and inventors. And that is indeed my impression of the British civil service. It is a beautifully designed and effective braking mechanism. It produces a hundred well-argued answers against initiative and change. To adapt the words of an old popular song, it accentuates the negative. If the positive forces — the forces of creativity and innovation and enterprise — were powerful, as they were in the late eighteenth and early nineteenth century Britain, it would be the best civil service that could be devised. Indeed, it was; full credit to the historical perceptions of Northcote and Trevelyan. But Northcote and Trevelyan did not foresee the loss of Britain's manufacturing and engineering vitality (although the first intimations were already there in the 1850s). So Britain has a civil service that could bring a Rolls Royce or a Cadillac to a stop within seconds, in a country with a two-horse engine power. The imbalance between the negative forces in Britain and the positive ones lies at the centre of our problems; and the civil service is the most effective of the negative ones.

Does that mean, then, that power resides in the civil service? Not, I think, wholly. Let me now explore the alternative analyses of the relationship between Ministers, civil servants and Parliament that are commonly presented.

The orthodox constitutional doctrine is clear. It is that Ministers are responsible to Parliament, and through Parliament's elected representatives, to the people, for everything that happens in their department. Second, Ministers share collective responsibility for the actions of the government, whether or not those actions relate to the Minister's own department. These doctrines are the core of Cabinet government. It is the collective responsibility of the Cabinet to Parliament that determines the role of the Prime Minister as *primus inter pares* — neither a president, a chief nor a king. Without the support of his Cabinet, the Prime Minister cannot in practice continue to govern; without the support of Parliament, he is constitutionally unable to do so.

One has only to state the first proposition, that Ministers are responsible to Parliament for everything that happens in their departments, to perceive that it cannot actually be the case. It is a doctrine which by its very nature cannot coincide with reality. If it ever did so coincide, it may have done so in some of the nineteenth century administrations that followed the two later reform bills — those of Derby and Disraeli or of Gladstone. In the past century, government has grown enormously, in the range of matters it concerns itself with, in the amount of money it spends, and in the volume of its communications with the public at large and with special interest groups in particular. The number of letters any large department deals with runs to several thousands a day, not to add in telephone calls. There is a pretty constant dialogue between a department and each of its major clients, and a more intermittent one between it and pressure groups on a particular national or local issue. In the nineteenth century, communications would have been limited to a relatively narrow subsection of a much smaller propulation.

It is simply impossible to believe that a Minister can oversee two or three thousand letters and communications going to and coming from the world outside each day, or that he or she could personally take the dozens of individual decisions that make up much of a department's work. For instance, the Home Office deals with hundreds of cases involving the granting of parole, or the placing of offenders in open rather than closed prisons every year. The Department of Education has numerous appeals from parents against being refused the right for their child to attend the school of their choice. The Department of Health looks into complaints by patients about their treatment by a particular hospital. The Minister will see the most difficult of these cases, where a tricky decision is involved, perhaps calling into question the administration of a health authority or a local education authority, or involving strongly held public views. He or she will also be expected to answer Parliamentary Questions on any of these individual cases, should an MP decide to raise it. In theory, the Minister will know all about why the parent's choice of school was overridden, or the offender was placed in an open prison rather than a closed one — but he or she will be entirely dependent in fact on knowledge gained at second hand from officials.

In the light of the growing responsibilities of government, the doctrine of individual ministerial responsibility is becoming less and less credible anyway, but three recent developments undermine it further. The first of these is that the press, radio and television have become much more aware of the internal workings of government departments, of their internal and external relations, and of the influence of individual civil servants upon departmental policy than was the case a decade ago. Journalists frequently meet and entertain senior civil servants and may establish close relations with them — what

Tony Benn described in his recent stimulating lecture as "this delicate briefing of top opinion-formers". Any reasonably sophisticated Minister can learn a good deal about what Whitehall thinks of him from the early profiles appearing in the newspapers as he takes over his new department.

Furthermore, newspapers in recent years have published government documents, confidential memoranda, committee papers classified as restricted, and even private correspondence on public issues, some of which were almost certainly obtained from civil servants. Indeed the determined struggle to uphold the secrecy of British government and administration, a struggle waged by senior civil servants and supported by many Ministers, is doomed as much by the media's existing access to much classified material as by parliamentary pressures for open government. In the USA, long before there was a Freedom of Information Act, the *New York Times* and other newspapers extensively printed sections of government documents given to them by officials serving the government of the day. Despite the Official Secrets Act, those who want to find means of publicizing government decisions or government policies-in-the-making can do so, because it becomes absurd to prosecute a newspaper for publishing material no one could possibly describe as threatening the security of the State. Many recent cases spring to mind: the publication of the so-called Yellow Paper on education, the source of the Prime Minister's speech shortly preceding the "great debate" of 1976; the instructions by the Home Office on how to deal with immigrants; documents on planning procedures and on teacher supply; and even, on rare occasions, alleged Cabinet or Cabinet Committee papers.

The second important area where the pressures are growing is within Parliament itself. I shall come on a bit later to the proposed reforms of Parliament, but even before those reforms are actually brought forward, it is evident that Parliament, partly because the quality of back-benchers has improved, and partly because more parliamentarians are full-time than used to be, is much more anxious to pursue what it regards as things that have gone wrong and is much more anxious to get select committees looking into government departments. (Relaxed knights from the shires and older trade union organizers have lost ground to lecturers, teachers and other professional people. The education profession now constitutes the largest single group of MPs.) MPs are much more likely to measure themselves in terms of the contributions they make to debates, the number of Parliamentary Questions they put down and so on, than was the case a generation ago.

I once fought a Member of Parliament, a most distinguished gentleman who had been re-elected through four different elections and whose only known recorded comment in the House of Commons was to ask if the windows might be closed. I do not believe that today an MP would escape censure by his constituency association or his constituency party if that was his sole contribution to Parliament. The number of written questions put down, the number of weekly oral questions put down, the requests for Private Members' time, the number of people seeking to get debates after 10 o'clock, all have multiplied over the last fifteen years and there is no sign that they are likely to decrease.

Third, but not least important: we clearly have, partly as a result of mass secondary education, a very much less resigned public than we used to have. It is quite interesting to look at the difference in the amount of constituency post that Members of Parliament get, depending upon what sort of constituency they represent. Generally speaking, if an MP represents a new town or suburb for example, his or her constituency correspondence will be of the order of two to four hundred letters a week. If he or she represents either a safe old-shire constituency as a Conservative or a safe north-eastern industrial seat as a Labour Member of Parliament, constituency correspondence is likely to be about one-quarter, maybe fifty or a hundred letters a week. Now the difference is not just the traditional difference between a fairly resigned part of the country, a part of the country that isn't used to things changing much or happening much. It is also a generational difference. Younger constituents are much more likely to make demands, much more likely to cut up rough if they do not get what they want, much more likely to hit the roof about the fact that their children have been allocated to the wrong school or their house is in a poor state of repair than their parents or grandparents were wont to do.

Let me simply take the fifteen years I was a Member of Parliament. I think in that time my constituency correspondence increased something like three times over, to the point of becoming virtually insupportable in terms of my ability to answer it on the basis of only one full-time secretary. Now very many are the signs of this: the number of requests for public inquiries, the ways in which those public inquiries attract all sorts of local groups and special interest groups, often very well-informed people, the amount of money that is put into resisting the coming of motorways, or new housing develop-ments, the way in which requests to override local authority decisions have increased very sharply, for instance in my old Ministry, the Department of Education. There is all sorts of evidence to show that we have a much more keen, much more enthusiastic, much more activist, much less easily satisfied public than we used to have. And we also have a public where people in a relatively under-privileged situation in society, for example, claimants for supplementary benefit or unemployment benefit, use their right to involve their Member of Parliament — and that means in turn a government department — in asking why they have not been properly treated by the civil service, or by the Minister, as the case may be. So, there is more press attention, more parliamentary pressure, and a less resigned public. And all that is good. But these things multiply the work of departments and multiply the areas for which the Minister is theoretically responsible. And so I am going to sum up the orthodox constitutional doctrine by saying that I myself believe it is reaching the end of its ability to be sustained as a constitutional fiction. It is a convenient constitutional fiction. For a democracy it is an attractive constitutional fiction. But the fiction is overtaking the attraction and I do not think myself that we will see it last very much longer.

Now the alternative thesis is that bureaucracy rules, and I have already mentioned some grounds for believing it. Let me dismiss the constitutional fiction about ministerial responsibility and take the opposite paradigm. There is a strong section of opinion in both the major political parties and, for all I know, in the Liberal Party as well, that believes the civil service in a tactful, delicate, largely hidden way runs the country. One can sum it up in terms of a cartoon that was recently carried in *The Guardian*, illustrating a slashing attack on the civil service by my erstwhile colleague Mr. Michael Meacher: there was a drawing of a very large car, which was filled with pin-striped senior civil servants (presumably most of them Permanent

Secretaries) and in front, sitting on the bonnet clutching a toy steering wheel, was the Minister, who was being driven about by the gentlemen inside the car. He clearly was under the happy illusion that he was driving the car, rather in the way that small children of two can be persuaded that that stick-on steering wheel is actually in control. The view that bureaucracy rules is the view that Ministers are essentially an elected figleaf, and that there is a complicated conspiracy to do them down and to destroy their policies. (The first of these propositions, though not the second, does command some support among civil servants themselves.) This view was put by Michael Meacher in an article that ought not to be dismissed, though I wouldn't myself agree with it all.

The first argument he put forward was that the civil service manipulates individual Ministers and it does so by the simple process of flattering them. Now it is perfectly true that the minute you become a Minister you normally cease to have a name, and you certainly cease to have a christian name, and you begin to be called by a title. Ergo, you are known as Parliamentary Secretary or sometimes briefly as "puss", when you first start your ministerial career. That doesn't addle the brain too much because it's a rather contemptuous term and you know it perfectly well if you are a "puss" or a Parliamentary Under-Secretary, the lowest form of ministerial life. There again the fiction — and this really is fiction — is that Parliamentary Secretaries and Permanent Secretaries are on an equal level of power, and that a locked argument between them can only be broken by somebody who is a Minister of State or a Secretary of State. (I once went away on holiday and came back to find my Parliamentary Secretary, who was a rather stroppy Parliamentary Secretary, and my Permanent Secretary, who did not think much of X's experience, locked in total combat on four different issues. Both of them had held up these decisions waiting for somebody to break the logjam, and in constitutional theory only a Secretary of State could break that logjam.)

Then you move up, and are called Minister of State or even Secretary of State. This always seems to me to be an extremely cumbrous title. Sentences of the form "ABC comma Secretary of State comma ABC" become very long. It is important that one does not get addicted to being called Secretary of State, to being treated with deference, and to being treated with great politeness. It is perfectly true that Ministers can be flattered, not least by these impressive appellations, but if so, the blame lies with the Minister, not with the civil service.

A second argument is that Ministers are isolated, that they are far less part of the network than the civil service is, and that therefore they can be pushed and persuaded into not adopting policies the department is not happy with or into adopting policies the department wants them to adopt, because they are lonely people and they are assailed from all sides by very strong and powerful arguments. It is true that Ministers are almost, though not quite, alone in their department, and that senior Ministers often have to take the most difficult decisions by themselves. But it is open to senior Ministers to discuss policies and tactics with their junior colleagues. All departments have at least one junior Minister, and most have three or more. These are party colleagues, concerned about the success of the government because they are seen as sharing responsibility for its achievements and its failures. Since Harold Wilson's first administration, Ministers can also employ a maximum of two advisers, men and women personally close to them, selected by the Minister, and almost invariably of his own political outlook. These advisers have been valuable eyes and ears for the Minister, and also create a useful network of communication between the Minister and the department, and between the Minister and the party, in Parliament and outside. Ministers also spend about half their lives in the House of Commons which often, ludicrously, means that they sit up half the night; there is nothing to stop them walking down corridors in a beehive which consists entirely of their colleagues who are also Ministers or MPs. So Ministers do not need to be isolated; if they are isolated it is either because they have decided to be isolated, or because the colossally heavy load of departmental papers on which decisions have to be made each night simply precludes them from taking time off for consultation and conversation. It is of course quite possible to pull your department round you like a blanket and keep the world out. In other words, it is possible to be cosseted within the capsule of the department in such a way that you do not actually want to put your ideas or your views, or your department's ideas and views, forward for the criticism or the comments of your fellow Ministers or MPs. But this is a self-defeating approach for a Minister, though not an unknown one.

One way of breaking down this sense of isolation is to create a large number of ministerial committees. Towards the end of the last Government, I think I was serving on about twenty separate Cabinet Committees of one kind or another, in which I constantly met the same fellow Ministers. If I had not been able to get to know their thinking pretty well and they to know mine, I would have been spending my time in an extremely unconstructive way. Now a lot of ministerial committees tends to create a circle of Ministers which parallels the official committees' circle of officials, and so you get two balancing systems in effect where everybody meets everybody else in a familiar circle. If you reduce the number of ministerial committees, as I believe Mrs. Thatcher is doing, you may get a balance in which the official committees become more important and become the hub of government, rather than the ministerial committees. Alternatively, you may get a strong inner-Cabinet structure in which the Prime Minister and a few chosen people around him or her become, in effect, the major decision-makers.

The striking thing about British government is that the Cabinet is a very flexible concept. Almost anything is possible, from the rather presidential style of government which Mr. Heath adopted at one stage in his administration, to a highly collective form of government, in which the Cabinet really does make the big decisions. I would not, however, so characterize the administrations in which I served on the Cabinet. They, I think, were characterized by an informal inner Cabinet, of perhaps three or four people gathered around the Prime

Minister. The individuals might be different according to the issue under discussion, but for most of the major decisions they would be the same.

So there is a very considerable spectrum of government styles that is possible in Britain because of an unwritten constitution. What has been interesting to me is that at least until very recently (and we cannot possibly judge yet where the present Government is going) there has been a move back from the presidential style of government. This may be because the concept of a government identified with one person is unsupportable because the pressures are becoming so great. What I have already said about ministerial responsibility in the department could be said also about presidential government in a very large country like the United States. However, I cannot pursue that because I am not talking about American government here.

Typically, as I have said, Cabinet Committees in Britain consist of Ministers, with a civil servant as secretary, and the official committees which underpin them consist of civil servants. Mixed committees of Ministers and civil servants are rare, though they do exist. I served on one in the 1960s which concerned itself with science and technology. It may be, as the Canadians have found, that mixed committees create a better relationship between Ministers and civil servants and one in which constitutional responsibilities are more clearly defined. Such mixed committees have the great advantage of demonstrating to Ministers that there are differences of view between officials and between departments; and inability to agree is not a genetic trait of the ministerial breed.

A third argument put forward in Tony Benn's stimulating recent lecture is that Whitehall can be mobilized against what an individual Minister may want to do by manipulating the inter-departmental framework. I believe there is some truth in that. Obviously an interdepartmental framework of committees, both ministerial and official, cannot be dispensed with. Most Cabinet decisions, and many departmental ones, have repercussions that go far beyond one department. The inter-departmental framework is very powerful; it does mean that a Minister in a particular department can be effectively blocked or constrained by the reactions of other departments. I myself have seen quite a lot of memoranda from other departments which say, "you should come down against Mr. or Mrs. So-and-So's proposals, because they would mean A, that your budget is cut because they are going to be expensive, or B, they are going to create considerable administrative strains, or C, they're not going to interest you anyway because it's not your department". So a very enterprising or very bold Minister can be stopped through the inter-departmental framework. But the Minister will certainly overcome any such obstruction if he or she has the backing and confidence of the Prime Minister and the

Cabinet. Tony Benn is absolutely right in saying that "if the Prime Minister retains real personal confidence in the Ministers whom he or she appoints, then the permanent secretaries know it is in their interest to support them" — and, of course, vice versa. Civil servants are after all human, and if they believe their Minister has embarked upon a foolish or unwise policy, and if they further believe it will not command Cabinet or prime ministerial support when it becomes known, they cannot really be blamed for not putting a great deal of effort into it.

However, the inter-departmental framework itself has considerable strains within it. It is not by any means the case that Whitehall, any more than Westminster, presents — except to the most undiscriminating eye — a solid front. For example, the strain between the Treasury and spending departments is always there. It can become very acute, especially at times of public expenditure cuts. That is a strain which any department that knows its way around recognizes, a ripple in the smooth inter-departmental surface. Again there are always ripples in the inter-departmental surface because departments traditionally adopt rather different attitudes about particular aspects of policy. To take one instance of this: protectionism versus free trade. There are almost automatically different attitudes between the Department of Trade, which has traditionally been a free trade department and still is to a very great extent, and the Department of Industry or the Department of Employment, which have a considerable tendency towatds protection-ism because of the nature of their clients and because of what they can see happening to the clients in certain situations where trade is totally unconstrained and where their clients are losing out in consequence.

So the inter-departmental framework is by no means as smooth a surface as Ministers sometimes believe it to be, especially in their first few years. For example, if a policy that is particularly cherished by a department is threatened by opposition from another department or by the Treasury, the department will do everything in its power, in support of its Minister, to defend the policy or to fight for it; and in my experience that alliance will hold through both official committees, ministerial committees and the Cabinet itself, though it may not prevail. Departments judge Ministers by how hard they fight, not so much with, as for, the department. One measure of their determina-tion is of course success — in getting the policy through or the expenditure cuts averted or reduced. But it is not the sole measure; Whitehall has a remarkable bush telegraph system, and word soon gets back to a department about how its Minister has acquitted himself on the battlefield. Furthermore, Ministers and departments may find common cause against another department, either because it is muscling in on their territory (what Americans call "turf disputes") or because of traditional differences of the kind mentioned above. Depart-

ments can create informal alliances; and so can Ministers. If the
Ministers and the Permanent Secretaries all work closely together, a
good deal can be achieved.

Reference was also made by Tony Benn to civil servants restricting
and controlling relevant information. This seems to me a very crude
way of trying to gain control over a Minister. In my view any
Minister worth his or her salt ought not to put up with it. It is a
question of remembering to keep asking for the same information and
when you have asked three times and had nothing, hitting the roof
in a structured sort of way. Hitting the roof in a structured sort of
way is something that Ministers should only do occasionally, and
they should always do it as a form of dramatic acting and not
because they have actually lost their temper (which will almost
invariably mean they lose out).

A more subtle form of obstruction is to take the Minister's instructions and then simply to do nothing. Ministers rarely have time to
progress-chase their smaller decisions. Unless the matter is bound to
come up again, a Minister's decision may just get itself lost. If the
Minister does recall his decision, administrative error or clerical
misfiling provide handy excuses. One of the main benefits of having
political advisers is that they can act as progress-chasers for the
Minister and prevent decisions losing themselves.

While I would want to qualify what the critics have said on these
points, on two arguments I find myself in agreement. It depends very
much what department you are in whether advice tends to take a
monolithic form or tends to take a collegiate form. Let me explain
what I mean. Advice that tends to take a monolithic form — and, for
example, I found that when I was in the Home Office advice tended
to take a monolithic form — is advice which grows like a tree. People
contribute to the brief as it goes up towards the Minister, but dissenting
opinions are gradually knocked out so that in the last two or three
stages from Assistant Secretary, Under Secretary to Deputy
Secretary — or if it is an extremely important policy, from Under
Secretary, Deputy Secretary to Permanent Secretary — all dissenting
views disappear from the files and what you are left with finally is the
official view.

Now, if you are a Minister the monolithic structure of advice (it has
been, I think, characteristic of the British civil service that the
structures have been mainly monolithic) is extremely irritating. What
it says to you is, "Minister, you either accept or reject this advice,
but if you reject this advice you are on your own. You're going to be
doing so without any structure of thought, without any structure of
fact, without any structure of advice. But of course if you want to do
it, Minister, you may do it — more fool you." Now, generally
speaking, in a monolithic advice pattern the only basis upon which

the Minister can reject the advice that he has received is by saying: "There are political considerations here which override". It is not untypical of the relationship between Ministers and the civil service that some civil servants feel the only proper basis for a Minister to disagree with official advice is by pleading political reasons or — dare I say — political dogma. Speaking as a Minister, I find that extremely unattractive. I do not believe that Ministers should overrule only on grounds of political dogma. I believe they should overrule because what they have seen of society or the world outside leads them to reach different conclusions, which may not be necessarily coloured by political partisanship, about the advice that they are offered. And so I much prefer the collegiate structure and I suspect it is going to be the structure that will increasingly be adopted.

The collegiate structure has been typical anyway in recent years of the Foreign Office, and is increasingly being accepted by domestic departments as well. Ministers get a number of policies put before them — options, if you like — each of them argued forcibly by different civil servants, where the Minister can call a meeting in which people are free to express different views upon which would be the best policy to answer the problem, and in which the Permanent Secretary or the Deputy Secretary will not delicately indicate his disapproval of a point of view different from his own. If the Minister is going to consider also parliamentary pressures and public concern, and balance out the different pressures on the department, then collegiate advice is a much more democratic kind of structure and generally speaking leads to better conclusions. We all know there have been pieces of monolithic advice that have been devastatingly wrong. The great danger of monolithic advice is that it gets rid of internal criticism to the point where there is only one argument that is able to be taken on board. It is a very dangerous situation for the highest levels not to go through the argument even if at the beginning they know what conclusions they think they want to reach.

Agendas for Cabinet or Cabinet Committee meetings can be a further instrument of control. Here again the problem is one both for Ministers and for the civil service, except for those very particular civil servants who become Secretaries to the Cabinet or members of the Cabinet Office. It is of course true that control of a Cabinet or Cabinet Committee agenda effectively gives one much closer control over the policy structures than would be the case if the Cabinet agenda were rather more flexible than it is. There is no "any other business" on a Cabinet agenda, amazingly, and therefore no room to take on board last-minute crises. Admittedly the forty-eight hour rule, that is to say that all papers are supposed to have forty-eight hours' notice given to them, is quite often broken; but the discretion to do so is that of the Cabinet Secretary. Therefore considerable power rests with the Prime Minister and the Secretary of the Cabinet, and sometimes with what I described earlier as the inner Cabinet. Whether it is necessary to control agendas to that extent, I would beg to leave to doubt.

I do not myself believe in either the traditional constitutional doctrine about ministerial responsibility nor in the more modern opposed doctrine that bureaucracy rules. After a good deal of thought, I have come to the conclusion that power consists of intersecting rings; it resides in the areas where people are able to come together between the civil service, Ministers, and to some extent a third group I am going to come to in a moment, pressure groups. Pressure groups are least looked at in constitutional literature. Though they are absolutely critical, they are the least investigated, and the least examined, even by the press, television and radio.

But before I come to pressure groups, I want to say what I *do* think is true about the civil service. In my experience, it is simply wrong to describe the civil service as a collectivity as being either pro-Conservative or pro-Socialist. It is obviously standard practice when a Labour Government comes in for one to say that the civil service is Conservative, and when a Conservative Government comes in, for them to say that the civil service is touched with leftist views. Why is it that both parties say this and say this with such conviction?

What is often underestimated is the extent to which departments have characteristics and indeed even characters. Departments are to a very great extent coloured in their attitudes by the last major reform that they undertook. The last great achievement is written on a department's banner and will be defended. If you consider a department like the Department of Health and Social Security, its last great monumental achievement in health was the National Health Service and its last great monumental achievement in pensions was the superannuation scheme; so the department understandably defends these great changes, and, in consequence, is obstructive towards Ministers who want to destroy those structures. Therefore one can say, if one is a Conservative, that the DHSS has a tendency to seem to defend Labour Government achievements rather than Conservative Government achievements. It is notable that, for example, the DHSS in the 1970-74 Government was extremely obstructive towards the idea of cost-related prescriptions which was at that time Sir Keith Joseph's policy, because they regarded cost-related prescriptions as likely to have a very damaging effect on the National Health Service. If I take my old department, the Department of Education and Science, that went through a complete transformation. In the '50s and early '60s it characteristically defended the achievements of the 1944 Education Act. It was what was written on its banner, so to speak. More recently, as the comprehensive reform came in, the department tended to defend comprehensive reorganization against those who objected to it or wished to turn it back. Equally if one looks at the Home Office, one sees a department which to my mind at least is very dominated by the considerations of those who are in charge of law and order, and therefore it tends to be a "Conservative department" when it comes to major changes and major reforms.

One can pursue this argument quite a long way, but basically it does seem to me that departments have these inner characteristics. It is not insignificant that if you go to the Department of Employment, which used to be called the Department of Labour, you move into a department many of whose senior officials work in shirtsleeves, and which tends to have a twenty-four hour time-scale because it is used to dealing with strikes, and tends to be close to, and sympathetic to, the trade unions. If you go to the Department of Industry, people dress differently, they are not so often in shirtsleeves, they have a slightly longer time-scale because they are concerned with industrial investment, and they are very close to the CBI and to industrial interests. So you cannot divorce departments both from their major achievements and from the pressure groups and the interest groups that surround them.

I would express the criticism that departments are always at the risk of getting too close to their particular interest groups or pressure groups. For many years MAFF has been very close to the farmers. MAFF is not a good department for determining the public interest; it is a very good department for determining the agricultural interest, not always the same thing. This was demonstrated, for example, by the position agricultural Ministers tended to take in Common Market negotiations, as exemplified not only in this country but in many others. Again, if one takes a department like Industry, Industry tends to be a soft department when it comes to anti-trust legislation, when it comes to monopoly and merger policy, and tends to find itself locked in combat with a department like the Department of Prices and Consumer Protection, now again merged with Trade, which used to be characteristically an anti-monopoly, anti-mergers department, with great suspicion about what would be the effect of monopolies and mergers on the consumer interest.

By the same token, new departments are likely to be more innovative than old ones. The short-lived Department of Economic Affairs was a highly innovative, indeed radical, department. It was regarded by the Treasury with all the suspicion and distrust of the elderly and well-established. DPCP also had a great willingness to try out new ideas: witness the open, competitive appointment to one of its most significant posts, that of Director-General of Fair Trading. But new departments have their work cut out to survive their infancy.

Begotten by ministerial whim or ministerial purpose, they are not often warmly nurtured by Whitehall. They get the best and the worst. To them go a handful of exceptional civil servants who are attracted by the challenge; to them are also sent those other departments want to lose.

But the final point I want to make about pressure groups and interest groups is that they are of course far less liable to come under the scrutiny of either Parliament or the press than the civil service is, or Ministers are. This to my mind is the great gap in the structure of British government. I strongly believe that the pressure groups and interest groups ought to be more effectively investigated and explored by the press. There is a characteristic of British government which I suspect is now becoming counter-productive. The civil service and Ministers constantly meet with and see various interest groups, which may be a professional association, or a trade union, or an industrial group. There is a very wide range of them as all of you appreciate. That pressure group or interest group will do everything in its power to amend or alter policy, usually in its own interest. If the department then amends or alters its policy in order to meet the demands of that interest or pressure group, the interest or pressure group never takes any responsibility for what it has done. It is the Minister and the department that then bear the responsibility.

Let me give an example. In the Plowden Report of 1967, there was a proposal that would have made it possible to bring about virtually full-scale nursery education in this country by employing nursery assistants trained for six months on NNEB courses to work under the supervision of qualified teachers. The Plowden Committee proposed that qualified teachers should be in charge of a group of nursery classes, perhaps four or five, each one of which would be staffed by nursery assistants, trained on a much more brief basis and less highly salaried obviously than the full-time primary teacher. There is no doubt that this proposal was popular with parents, was popular with the Government, and would have been adopted had there been an open relationship going. But the professional associations opposed it on the grounds that they wanted to see no move towards a dilution of professional responsibility for nursery classes, i.e. there must be a fully qualified nursery teacher in charge of each nursery class. Now this in effect meant that the Plowden proposal could not go ahead because it was simply too expensive to put a fully qualified primary school teacher in charge of each nursery class. But the Government never gave the reasons why it did not go ahead or put the difference before the forum of public opinion.

To this very day in government we tend to protect interest groups from what would be considerable public pressure if the public knew the extent to which certain groups had been able to amend and alter policy by saying they would not co-operate unless it was amended or altered. My view is that this ought to be brought out into the open, and that if it were, we would have a more effective, more democratic and more "public interest" kind of administration than we have at the present time.

But I recognize that this view may be wrong. A distinguished US expert on British government — and on US government — remarked that interest groups might have to be even more intransigent and hard-nosed if their leaders' submissions were all made public.

That brings me to the relationship of the civil service to Parliament. Parliament is in many ways an emotional place. It is a place which tends to react very much to general policies and general principles. The careful preparation that the civil service gives to Parliamentary Questions, to parliamentary debates and to inquiries by select committees, often reflects a certain lack of empathy with the way in which Parliament thinks and Parliament reacts. Generally speaking, no experienced Minister would make the mistake of simply reading out a speech to Parliament written by a civil servant unless he were under great pressure of time. Those very painstaking answers to supplementary questions which civil servants spend a great deal of time on are rarely of much use. I can guarantee that if a Minister answers a parliamentary debate or a Parliamentary Question along the lines prepared for him he will not make a dreadful mistake, but he will certainly never have any kind of parliamentary triumph. The reason for this is that what civil servants think that Parliament wants is either an argument for why you are doing what you are doing, or a clear indication of what your policies are and where they are going. What happens is that the wood is lost in the trees, and that the job of Ministers is to put back the wood.

Civil servants are extremely conscientious about Parliament. They spend a great deal of time on it, and they are often rather disappointed in the level of knowledge that Members of Parliament actually bring to a particular departmental field of interest. Very often when I looked at the faces in the box, I could see that they were — shattered is too strong a word — certainly rather disappointed or disillusioned in the level of debate they were encountering. One reason for this is that Parliament is so badly staffed. I would be the last person to want to see the ludicrous staffing levels that we now see in the US Congress, which on last count had 13,000 administrative and legal assistants to congressmen and to committees. This means that the administrative assistants, as they are now doing, begin to take over from the congressmen. It is very interesting that at many meetings of congressional committees, aides outnumber elected officials. It is a dangerous way for democracy to go. But at the other end, the British Parliament is so seriously understaffed that Members of Parliament are constantly flying on the seat of their pants, in select committees and other places. There is a balance to be struck between the two.

We are going to see in the next few years three developments in respect of Parliament itself. There are twelve select committees and each shadows a department. Those select committees will demand increased staffing and that will create a counter-civil service. It will be much smaller obviously than the civil service. It probably will not constitute more than half a dozen members of staff for each select committee. But even given that, the quality of parliamentary questioning, or parliamentary inquiry, is likely to be very much higher in the next ten years than it has been at any time in the past.

Secondly, as we begin to get some kind of official freedom of information act — and it is as certain as my standing here that we will in the course of, if not the next Parliament, then the one after — there will be much more information made available not only to Members of Parliament but above all to the press. The classification categories known as "confidential" and "restricted" have become absurd. The "restricted" category means what we can read in the *Daily Telegraph* or *The Guardian*. The "confidential" category means what we are going to read in *The Guardian* and the *Daily Telegraph* tomorrow. The only set of categories which are worth having are the "secret" and "top secret" categories, incidentally often over-classified. I have seen all sorts of things called "secret" which should not be, and what I think we shall need to do, given the Official Information Act, is to look very carefully at the ways in which things are classified. The great danger is to simply over-classify all kinds of information in order to bring it back within the protection of the Official Secrets Act; to do that, in my view, would simply force yet another set of official information acts until we finally end up with the legislation that the United States now has, which goes — again in my view — a bit too far in terms of undermining the protection of individual records and the protection of individual people. So there will be the select committees, more expert staff, official information acts, removing in effect the "restricted" and "confidential" categories.

Parliamentary select committees are bound increasingly to question civil servants, not just about future legislation but about the formulation of policy and its execution at national and local level. Indeed, this is a clear consequence of recognizing the true limits of ministerial responsibility. Ministers will not be able to answer over the whole range of questions; the areas in which they have actually made the decisions and the areas in which they have not will become more and more evident. I expect the doctrine of direct ministerial responsibility will then shrink to its real size, responsibility for the major policies and objectives of the Minister's particular government. Since Parliament will not allow the other, more detailed administrative decisions to go unquestioned, civil servants will find themselves being held responsible for them, albeit that their constitutional accountability to the Minister may remain. At the very least, Parliament if unsatisfied will expect the Minister to make his own inquiries and report his own conclusions. Personally, while I recognize that there is some risk of politicizing — or appearing to politicize — civil servants, it is a risk in my view worth running in order to get more effective accountability for the work of government departments, not least as they impinge upon the individual citizen. But perhaps the new line should run between policy formulation and its execution, with Ministers continuing to be held responsible for the former, and crucially political, area.

There is another possible parliamentary reform which has been much less discussed and that is providing an opportunity for parliamentary debate of longer-term changes in our society. In his lecture, Tony Benn referred to the civil service's "deep commitment to the benefits of continuity and a fear that adversary politics may lead to sharp reversals by incoming governments of policies devised by their predecessors which the civil service played a great part in developing". He concludes that "this central theme of consensus or Whitehall policies which have been pursued by all parties for the last 20 years or so have been accompanied by a steady decline in Britain's fortunes, which has now accelerated into a near catastrophic collapse of our industrial base".

I find this an extraordinary explanation of Britain's decline. Observers from outside the country, or from industry, are much more likely to comment on the ping-pong nature of British governments, constantly altering policies which have long-term consequences, than they are to observe the broad bland areas of agreement characteristic of consensus politics. Certainly there was something of a consensus in the fifties and early sixties; but even in those years industries like steel and road haulage were shuttlecocked back and forth between public and private ownership at a high cost in terms of efficiency. Investment incentives have changed time and again, as have regional policies; trade unions have been alternatively threatened with legislation and pay freezes, or cajoled into social contracts and voluntary income policies, all of them pretty short-term. The schools have remained a battleground between comprehensive and selective systems, in which some pathetic children, as in Thameside or Enfield, were compelled at the last minute to go through a selective process they and their parents believed had gone for ever.

Of course there must be argument, choice and change in politics, but British politics demonstrates a desperate neglect of the long term, and an almost total failure to involve Parliament, and through it the people, in debating where we are going and how we are to get there.

In contrast to Tony Benn, I would argue that it is precisely those areas which have long lead-times, such as industrial investment and scientific research, that have suffered most from U-turns and chopped and changed policies, many lacking any ideological characteristic of differences between the parties, but merely demonstrating a desire for Ministers and governments to stamp their personal image on policy making. I would favour the presence of the Leader of the Opposition on NEDC, so that he or she would be familiar with the views of the representatives of both the trades unions and the employers when the alternative party comes to office.

Of course it is vital that Parliament be involved in this process. In my view, no major legislation should ever come forward again without a Green Paper and a parliamentary debate on that Green Paper preceding it. In that way one might begin to build a degree of parliamentary support for long-term reforms which require time to develop. There ought to be a new stage in debate. The select committee shadowing the department responsible for a particular piece of legislation will want to hear, in advance of any bill being brought before Parliament, what is going to be in the bill, and to have an opportunity to question Ministers, and perhaps civil servants, about it. But that by itself is not enough. The second stage is also important: an actual parliamentary debate on the Green Paper in advance of major legislation, because one ought to have not only the internal interest of a well-informed select committee but the opportunity to consult the wider public interest, which will be represented in the debate by other Members of Parliament taking part. I would even hope that the select committee members would generally speaking be called only *after* Members of Parliament not on that select committee had had an opportunity to express their view.

In addition, Parliament should have time to debate the reports of major commissions and committees, not only those set up by government departments themselves, but the results of significant independent study or research as well. It is the more distant horizon that is singularly neglected by British politicians, and we have only ourselves to blame if a responsible and concerned civil service compensates for that neglect by providing its own continuities.

Discussion

A questioner suggested that the relative unresponsiveness of the civil service might be caused in the first place by its professionalism and, secondly, by the influence on it of pressure groups. Mrs. Williams agreed with both these points. She referred to her earlier remarks about the influence on a department's thinking of its last major reform, and suggested that the present Conservative administration might be having some difficulties in implementing its policies in the social service departments, just as the previous Labour administration had had some difficulties with the financial and monetary departments. Turning to the pressure groups, she suggested that there existed an "uneasy sweetheart relationship between the pressure groups and departments that sometimes not only makes it difficult for Ministers to take action but actually constrains the civil servants themselves, because of the attitudes of their colleagues who say, 'Don't rock the boat: this is going to be very difficult with such and such professional association or such and such an industry', and may therefore try to smooth the whole thing over even when it is a situation that is crying for change." She recalled a case where a very bad monopoly situation had been allowed to continue untouched because a department which had very close links with the firm in question did everything that it could to ensure that as little attention as possible was drawn to the embarrassing level of the firm's monopoly control — mainly because those in the department concerned wanted a reasonably quiet life.

A questioner asked about the problem of briefing Cabinet Ministers for discussions where the subject matter went beyond the department's interest and competence. Were there people in each department with enough breadth of knowledge to brief their own Ministers on such questions? If not, could or should Ministers be able to draw on briefing from the specialized departments directly concerned? Mrs. Williams replied: "I think it is a very interesting question, and if I could simply take for a moment a spectrum it would look like this. The closer to your departmental interest an item in Cabinet is — I am only speaking of my experience, obviously — the more significant the departmental administrative briefing is going to be, and as it moves further and further away from the department's own area of interest the more significant your purely political instincts or attitudes become. So that in a way you become enfranchized of the considerations the department brings to your attention by issues that fall very far outside your field. If we were discussing Rhodesia, I felt deliciously on my own and I could express what I thought and what I felt and what my gut reactions were, possibly in consultation with the only people who, in a sense, are then privy to that particular kind of briefing, which would tend to be one's political advisers. Indeed, I'd say one of the important functions of political advisers is that one tends to turn to them for advice outside the departmental framework. There is a special case of that and that is when the issue is not one totally separate from the department but what I can only describe as an utterly over-arching issue like should we devalue, should we retreat from the Himalayas.... And there again, I think that one would tend to move away from departmental advice except insofar as the department is directly affected by what flows from, say, devaluation.

"Now, with regard to your questions about would one like to have advice direct from the department concerned: no, I would very much not want to have that. You may say, because you'd rather live in a state where ignorance is bliss; I don't think so. I think in many ways one of the most effective roles of Cabinet is in a sense to put the detail of knowledge and understanding and commitment of a Minister to his department and his department's brief to the test; you cannot easily put it to the test if you yourself are no longer expressing the common reaction of other people in Parliament, or of the public, but are beginning to be coloured by the department's own set of attitudes. So I think your judgment would not be good. I think it would become a semi-professional judgment and that would be a bad thing. Last of all, the CPRS obviously crops up in this area and, yes, I think here I would go along with what I think lies behind your question. I wouldn't favour advice from the department concerned because that would colour the Cabinet's attitude very badly. I would accept the idea that the CPRS ought to be allowed to give advice to individual Ministers on the normal basis of not, obviously, trying to brief them against a particular Minister or particular set of things, but simply bringing forward the considerations that Ministers might want to have in mind in looking at this issue."

A civil servant commented: "Among the many criticisms which are levelled at the civil service, and have been during this series of talks, I think the only one which I really resent, and it is one which Mrs. Williams repeated this evening, is that civil servants are resistant to change and indeed incompetent to assist in the process of change. I don't think civil servants are resistant to change. It's one of the few things that makes their wretched lives interesting; if you're involved in it, it gives you a chance to make your mark. But when civil servants are confronted with proposals for change by Ministers, I think they ask themselves three or four kinds of questions. Firstly, practicality: will it work? Secondly, utility: if it looks workable, will it have the desired result? Thirdly, equity: is it fair to all the people who might be affected by the change? Fourthly, how much work will it involve? Now these considerations will sometimes impede ministerial desires for change and very often Ministers show very little concern for them. But is it not the civil servant's job to ask those questions and try to answer them?"

Mrs. Williams replied: "Yes. And I apologize because I was trying to make what I thought was a slightly more subtle point. Really what I was trying to say were three things. First of all, I don't think it is true to say, just like that, that civil servants obstruct change. I tried to say I don't believe that to be true. What I believe to be true is that it's very much easier for departments to take on changes that build on things they have already done, than to take on changes which destroy what they have already done. And I don't find that at all odd. It is much easier to edit a book than to tear it up and start writing again, especially if you are actually rather pleased with the book. It is easier to slightly alter one's upbringing of a child than actually to sort of say 'Well, that child's not much good, so I'll begin again'. What I'm trying to get at is that it simply is the case that the civil service department is more likely to work with you and be with you and help you with a full heart if you are building on the best of what that civil service department has already done. And if they didn't they would have no loyalty to either what they've already done or what their departments stands for. And that's why I was trying to make the point about what's 'blazoned on the banner'. It's a metaphor, if you like, but I think it's quite an important one. At least it's very much what I have felt in many, many different ministries, admittedly mostly on domestic side.

"The second point I was trying to make was that I think Parliament is partly at fault, and politicians, because I think we have not built in mechanisms for considering the desirability of changes against the background of the condition of the country. That's what I was pleading for: much more debate in Parliament and in government among political people on the nature and directions of long-term change. Because, if I may put it absolutely, it pains me profoundly that we should muck about with people in the way that we do by making sudden, often ill-thought-through changes which the other party says they will reverse when they get back into power, rather than trying to, in a sense, corral the genuine argument between politicians in certain fields and to see what one can agree on because there isn't an ideological rift about it. I would guess that if we pursued a consistent policy of investment allowances or initial allowances or investment grants over, say, ten years, we would have a much more satisfied business community, whether Labour or Conservative was in office, than we do by moving from one to the other at the dramatic speed of change, sometimes as little as two years, before the whole structure's altered. It isn't particularly socialist to have grants or allowances, or particularly conservative to have initial allowances rather than investment allowances, so I simply don't understand why we spend so much time changing the machinery for no special reason except for the pleasure of showing that you can do it. So I don't want to give the impression that I'm making a blanket comment that civil servants don't want change. I did make one blanket comment and I'll stand by it. I think that partly because it is a very good service, because it attracts very able people, because it still has a very high degree of dedication and discipline, that one has to recognize that by the nature of a civil service in any country in the world, the civil service is largely a negative force. You have to have positive and negative forces in a society; but in Britain, because an equal level of ability, talent, energy and creativity is not finding its way into industry or into the services other than the public services, the balance of society, in my view, has gone a bit awry and we are very good at regulating what isn't a sufficiently powerful machine to regulate."

A question was asked about the relationship between civil servants and Members of Parliament. The questioner suggested that each side was ignorant of and unsympathetic towards the other, and that civil servants were positively discouraged from having contacts with MPs. He wondered whether the new select committees might help to bring about closer relationships and, if so, whether Mrs. Williams would welcome this. Mrs. Williams said she would welcome it very much. It was very important that MPs should be able to talk to, inform and learn from people at the higher policy-making levels of the civil service. Although the new select committees might at first make the situation worse, after about six or twelve months it should begin to improve. "One will get people more readily learning from one another, civil servants discovering what it is that's bothering and troubling Members of Parliament, what the constituency input is to the way they think, the way they act, and I think eventually probably coming to have more respect for them — at least I hope so, because I think they will cease to be seen purely as political machines and more as people who are reflecting the attitudes and their responsibility to the public that they represent and serve. And vice versa: I think that civil servants will begin to realize that the process of Parliament asking questions could lead to a better informed and more influential Parliament. I am one of those who think that the balance between the executive and the legislature has gone very much too far towards the executive and I want to see the legislature strengthened and in the end I think it can only be strengthened by greater knowledge and greater awareness of what it's doing." However, Mrs. Williams did not want the legislature to become as "out of hand" as Congress in the United States. "The most immiserated civil service I've seen," she said, "is the US one, I think. I haven't spent much time in the Soviet Union — it may be worse there. I suspect it's much better."

Biographical Notes

The Rt. Hon. William Rodgers was elected Member of Parliament for Stockton-on-Tees in 1962. His first ministerial post was at the Department of Economic Affairs. In all, he has served as a Minister in six departments, including the Foreign Office, Treasury, Defence, and latterly from 1976-1979 as Secretary of State for Transport.

The Rt. Hon. Edmund Dell was MP for Birkenhead from 1964-79. His first ministerial posts were in the Ministry of Technology and the Department of Economic Affairs. He subsequently became Minister of State at the Board of Trade (1968-69) and the Department of Employment and Productivity (1969-70). His last government post was as Secretary of State for Trade from 1976-78. He was recently appointed Chairman of the Board of the new fourth television channel.

The Rt. Hon. Merlyn Rees was elected MP for Leeds (South) in 1963. Two years later he took up the first of two ministerial posts in the Ministry of Defence, followed by two years in the Home Office. After serving as Secretary of State for Northern Ireland from 1974-76, he returned to the Home Office as Secretary of State from 1976-79.

The Rt. Hon. Tony Benn was elected to Parliament in 1950 as Member for Bristol (South East). His early ministerial posts included Postmaster General, Minister of Technology and Minister of Power. He was appointed Minister of Posts and Telecommunications in 1974 and later became Secretary of State for Industry (1974-75) and for Energy (1975-79).

The Rt. Hon. Shirley Williams was MP for Hitchin from 1964-74 and for Hertford and Stevenage from 1974-79. Her first ministerial post was in the Ministry of Labour. She served as Minister of State in the Department of Education and Science (1967-69) and the Home Offce (1969-70). In 1974 she became Secretary of State for Prices and Consumer Protection and in 1976 Secretary of State for Education and Science. She has lectured at the Civil Service College and was a member of the Fulton Committee.